AF407844

Rana Eijaz Ahmad & Mahnoor Mansoor

GLOBALIZATION AND SYSTEM CAPABILITIES

China and India in the Twenty-First Century

Ledizioni

Rana Eijaz Ahmad & Mahnoor Mansoor, *Globalization and System Capabilities.*
China and India in the Twenty-First Century

First edition Ledizioni: March 2024
ISBN Print 9791256001033
ISBN eBook 9791256001040

Catalogue and reprints information: www.ledipublishing.com, www.ledizioni.it

Table of Contents

We dedicate this book to our beloved sons

Muhammad Abdullah Shahzad
and
Rana Ibrahim Ahmad

List of Abbreviations

AIIB (Asian Infrastructure Investment Bank)
ASEAN (Association for the South East Asian Nations)
BRI (Belt and Road Initiative)
CPEC (China Pakistan Economic Corridor)
CRR (Cash Reserve Ratio)
ECO (Economic Cooperation Organization)
EPZs (Export Processing Zones)
FDI (Foreign Direct Investment)
GDP (Gross Domestic Product)
GNP (Gross National Product)
IFIs (International Financial Institutions)
IMF (International Monetary Fund)
IOs (International organizations)
IT (information technology)
MNCs (Multinational Corporations)
MNGs (Multinational Governments)
NATO (North Atlantic Treaty Organization)
NITI (National Institution for Transforming India)
SAARC (South Asian Association for Regional Cooperation)
SLR (Statutory Liquidity Ratio)
SNT (Social Network Theory)
WHO (World Health Organization)
WMD (Weapons of Mass Destruction)
WTO (World Trade Organization)

Preface

Welcome to the world of artificial intelligence, where digitalization has transformed the globe worldwide. This book investigates the 'system capabilities' and its utilization through the lens of leadership as per its idiosyncrasy. The thesis of this book emphasizes that it is not the form of government but the efficient utilization of the system capabilities by the leadership that make the difference in the socio-political and economic development of any country in the world. It provides a dynamic landscape of globalization, discovering how two economic dynamos—China and India—navigate and shape the complicated web of global relations in the contemporary era.

As the world becomes increasingly interconnected, understanding the roles of major players in shaping global systems is crucial. China and India, with their rich histories, diverse cultures, and rapidly evolving economies, stand as pivotal actors in the unfolding narrative of our shared global future.

This book is not merely a survey of economic trends or geopolitical strategies. Instead, it seeks to unravel the intricate tapestry of system capabilities—how nations efficiently harness their resources, institutions, and social and human capital to prosper in the globalized world. Focusing on China and India, we aim to offer insights into contrasting political systems, approaches, challenges, and opportunities these countries encounter as they circumnavigate the complexities of a rapidly changing global environment and claim to have communism and the largest democracy, respectively.

The chapters within this volume traverse various topics, from economic policies and technological advancements to social dynamics, cultural influences, and environmental concerns. Through meticulous analysis and thoughtful exploration, we aim to provide a comprehensive understanding of the multifaceted dimensions that contribute to the global positioning of China and India.

Our journey unfolds against the backdrop of the twenty-first century—a period marked by unprecedented, ostensibly technological advancements, shifting geopolitical alliances, pandemics, and a growing awareness of nations' interdependence. As we explore the narratives of China and India, we invite readers to contemplate the broader implications for the global community and to reflect on the shared challenges and opportunities that create a borderless world.

This book is a collaborative effort, bringing together perspectives from scholars, experts, and thinkers dedicated to unraveling the complexities of globalization and system capabilities. We hope this exploration sparks curiosity, encourages critical thinking, and fosters a deeper understanding of the evolving global landscape.

As we embark on this cerebral venture, we invite readers to engage with the material, question assumptions, and consider the narratives' implications. Globalization and System Capabilities seek to contribute to the ongoing dialogue about the future of our interconnected world, and we are honored to have you as part of this conversation.

Happy reading.

Mahnoor Mansoor
27-01-2024

Introduction. Globalization and System Capabilities: China and India in the Twenty-First Century

By Rana Eijaz Ahmad, Mahnoor Mansoor

Introduction

This book is going to explain that it is not the form of government that is going to make any difference in the socio-political or economic life of any political system; these are the 'system capabilities' a leader exploits to develop a system. Therefore, the leader and leadership are at the top to utilize the 'system capabilities' as per its disposition and make the political system workable or semi-workable or keep it in a state of abeyance.

In every political system, group, family, tribe, or village, there are three types of individuals: parochial, subjects, and participants. The country that has more number participants may be more prosperous and developed. The composition of individuals keeps changing in different phases of the state's life. For example, suppose today there are more individuals of the subject' type in China and more parochial in India. In that case, they may become more participants in the future, but that depends on how the leader or leadership exploits the 'system capabilities' to sustain a workable political system.

Globalization is an old phenomenon with new technological advancements in the contemporary world. It has become the buzzword for the traditional and transitional democracies, totalitarian, authoritative dictatorships, monarchies, and fascists of the modern world. Still, it is a subject of serious study for social scientists. It is based on human welfare and the integration of the whole world. Increased interconnectedness, interdependence, and collectivism are used to define globalization.

Asia has been a multipolar region with numerous diverse civilizations that primarily evolved, irrespective of Western policies, yet managed tactfully to coexist with one another. In this book, two major Asian countries, China and India, will come under discussions that are entering the twenty-first century with a difference. They successfully face globalization's challenges and give other developing states a blueprint to follow suit. Viewing the world from an Asian lens divulges that the United States' role is more of a service provider than a hegemon. The United States is a vendor in the global market, whereas Asia has been its largest customer. Today, it is also a competitor. Historically, the United States was a default option to provide security, capital, and technology. Today, Asian countries are successfully providing these services to one another. Therefore, the United States is far more dispensable than it imagines.[1] The process of globalization made it possible.

Globalization is Multifaceted

Globalization is a process that makes economic, political, social, environmental, technological, and security concerns a well-knitted interconnected unit for the welfare of communities at national as well as international levels with its tools like the Multinational Corporations (MNCs), the (International Financial Institutions) IFIs, and the World Trade Organization) WTO. The political, economic, social, and other sub-state actors, like non-governmental organizations and civil society, collectively work for a tightly integrated society.

James H. Mittelman underscores that "globalization is not a single, unified phenomenon, but a syndrome of processes and activities.[2] It is a multifaceted and interdisciplinary phenomenon that interacts with all dimensions and deeply affects human activities. He further says that the word "syndrome" assigns a blueprint of interconnected characteristics of human circumstances, particularly within the global political economy. It (syndrome) is not concerned with the medical term related to disease indication as globalization is not unnatural or abnormal.[3] It is an increased interconnectedness of the countries, people, institutions, cultures, religions, and civilizations through the 'democratization of technology,' 'democratization of finance,' and 'democratization of information with the help of cyberspace, credit cards, and the internet respectively.[4]

Mittelman cites Giddens for an elaborate definition of globalization. "Globalization can thus be defined as the intensification of worldwide social relations which links distant localities in such a way that local happenings are shaped by events occurring many miles away and vice versa."[5]

Globalization is all macro-level economic activities, for example, Asia's "growth triangle," a term created by Singapore's Prime Minister Goh Chok Tong in 1989, and micro levels of projects such as export processing zones (EPZs) that starts from a state inside and goes beyond other satellites of this universe. These projects may be political, economic, social, environmental, nuclear, or based on any other human interaction directly or indirectly concerned with living organisms.

This document explores an exciting aspect of the great civilizations' challenge confronting the countries under discussion (China and India). These societies continuously strive to sustain their cultural outlook and secure their material and spiritual existence in the age of globalization. The impact of globalization on China and India will be measured in three significant aspects: economic, political, and social.

Another critical factor is that globalization is making an impact on the cultural values of these countries.[6] Despite countless developments, many domestic ills are still prevalent even in Western societies, such as mounting debt, social inequality, political polarization, ethnic wars, and declining median income.[7] It is also worth noting that there are no adequate checks on Asian MNCs. This immunity enables them to have a free hand in promoting environmental pollution. There have also been human rights violations in these countries. Hence, the impact of globalization in Asia is very selective, partial, and gloomy. Instead of being primitive, globalization has a somewhat distorted image of this part of the planet.

Tracing back to the 1990s, when China was intrigued by the idea of foreign capital, Chinese firms were subjected to intense global competition. Rural firms of China lagged in expertise and technology; therefore, the state was not well equipped to deal with the turbulence of global competition. Consequently, negative experiences based on flawed dealings with overseas competitors fostered nationalistic tendencies at these firms; instead of global economic convergence, Chinese firms became dependent on domestic markets. The loyal private capital was a significant factor in preserving and developing Communist autocracy in China.[8]

The impact of increased interconnectedness in China and India's economic, political, and social domains is based on duplicitous and contradictory policies. International financial institutions (IFIs) and multinational corporations (MNCs) ameliorate the economies on one hand and damage the overall local business on the other. This impact is also wide-ranging in India; for example, the MNCs in Bihar and Maharashtra are doing good business compared to Nagaland or Uttar Pradesh.

The liberalization process in India is encouraging social transformations. Since the return of substantial Diasporas to the homeland, India has opened to Western MNCs that renovated economic ideas such as the evolution of indigenous business and more support for FDI liberalization. Although counter-trends are still prevalent here, India's future liberalization cannot accommodate anti-FDI policies. Despite protectionist domestic interests, the thirty years of economic liberalization have made India a fruitful ground for foreign investments in the future.[9]

In the same way, the impact of globalization on China also has contradictions in their social, economic, and political domains. Expatriate Chinese and Taiwanese are the major investors in China. Under joint enterprises, the MNCs and local industries manufacture consumer goods jointly. Cars and mobile phones are produced in abundance. In the first phase of modernization, 24 special economic zones in China got attention. Shan Zen was a fishing area 20 years ago but has grown into an ultra-modern city. This modernization is taking place in China on the Pacific coast. Regional disparities are owing to the MNCs, the difference in the wage structure, and the lack of buying power. The second phase of modernization moves from the Pacific to the Western part of China on a large scale. It has increased corruption and prostitution in China. There may be a contradiction in political and economic reforms in the future. It concentrates on the prosperity of life, not human rights and democracy.

Paul Salopek, the National Geographic explorer, claims, "Asia is so huge and complex that I feel like I am moving through a vast mosaic of microworlds, loosely knitted together by forces beyond my ken." Although Asia is considered the most heterogeneous region of the world, the psychological underpinnings and cultural thread develop coherence at the regional level, making it unique comparatively. Historically, Asian civilizations maintained commercial ties from the Mediterranean to the Indus Valley. However, European colonization negatively influenced Asia. Subsequently, being subjected to competitive spheres of influence, the contemporary post-Cold War period has joined Asia into a unified system. Today's coherent system is a collection of geographically, diplomatically, and economically interconnected countries. Regardless of being sovereign and independent, members of the system are politically and economically interdependent. Alliances, institutions, security, trade, culture, and other similar patterns characterize the system.[10]

Asia has strategic importance in the community of nations. China and India must play an essential role in future regional policy designs. This is impossible if there is animosity between them. In the twenty-first century, China and India are supposed to settle their differences as early as possible. This is an age of revolutionizing communication and multimedia that has diminished the specific borders of nation-states. In other words, the "wiring of the world" allows every individual to look into every development emerging on this planet. Thus, It has become hard for governments to keep people ignorant of their policies. Consequently, China and India have to rethink their future.

System Capabilities

These are "system capabilities"[11] (this term is used by Gabriel A. Almond and G. Bingham Powell Jr. and may be used by other writers) and other internal sub-state actors that may make a difference in a country's socio-political and economic development. This book will also highlight how the political systems of the countries under discussion are intellectually dependent upon the developed world. It means that whatever is considered best for the West is good for the rest. Both countries' degrees of dependence vary, so the impact of globalization also varies. It is not uniform. For example, system capabilities are the major variant for both China and India.

It is asserted in this book that there is a more significant cultural and social impact of globalization on India rather than on China, but it is under threat, too. India is more robust in its democratic framework, unlike China, a communist regime, and successful in continuing its ideology, even in this age of globalization, where the market economy is the essence of free trade. Interestingly, Chinese civilization is carrying the world economy with its annual economic growth rate of 10.7% to 11%, the highest in the world. Its counterpart, India, being a democratic regime, is far behind China.

Irrespective of the perplexing enigma of adopting different paths of liberalization, the role of Diasporas in China and India cannot be ignored for uplifting the economies through foreign direct investment (FDI) reforms and forging changes in domestic business, respectively. Historical and contemporary emigration significantly contributed to shaping liberal policy, circulating human capital, and strengthening the ties of domestic business to global markets. However, the Chinese Diaspora superseded those of India to influence FDI liberalization.[12]

This manuscript will also expose that two different political systems are undergoing globalization with advantages and disadvantages. The political systems with more efficient 'system capabilities' by the leadership will survive. In contrast, others will disintegrate or configure with the countries with efficient leadership and 'system capabilities' sooner or later for a sustainable economy.

Kenichi Ohmae says that the country has no bar upon the flow of capital, goods, and services because of the revolution in communication. Information technology has diminished the frontiers of many nations, allowing them to overcome the world's economic market.[13]

The conventional political discourse has been globally transformed into a post-ideological landscape. Modern societies encourage an equilibrium of interconnectedness and security, individualism and interdependence, autonomy, and social welfare. Democracy is no longer attributed as a sole yardstick to measure prosperity; instead, the common masses are more concerned about openness, protection, and sustainable policies to ensure affluence.[14]

The Internet, cyberspace, e-mail, fax, Facebook, YouTube, WhatsApp, Twitter, and various multimedia extensions have rapidly increased the world's interconnectedness. Information technology is bringing political entities closer together. Scientific and technological advancement has made the world a complex amalgam of political and economic systems.

The new world information order is unilaterally spreading the Western and

European cultural onslaught of Asian and African countries. The communication revolution is permeating the developing countries. The cable network is showing Western and European channels. Although the Indian channels compete with the Western channels, they are inadequate.

It seems that India is fast westernizing its culture, and its traditional values are lagging in media representation. Imitating the TV channels instigates the masses towards acculturation that causes 'migration of dreams' (the impact on the poor of television programs emanating from wealthier societies) and 'relative deprivation (the gap between what one gets and what one thinks they should get). [15]China is also adopting modernization and doing its best to get more fruits of globalization. It seems successful due to its active "system capabilities." Under its modernization campaign, China emphasizes four sectors: agriculture, industry, defense forces, and science and technology. It follows two pragmatic objectives: first, to promote the cause of the multipolar world, and second, to contain and engage the United States of America.

Politically, Asia seems unstable due to its weak political institutions and low-profile "system capabilities." The system's capabilities may be enumerated as extractive, regulative, distributive, symbolic, and responsive.[16] According to Almond and Powell, extractive capability means that a political system should be able to extract its economic and natural resources at domestic and international levels. For example, collecting taxes at home and bringing more investments from abroad shows that extractive capability is active. Regulative capability is the regulation of resources extracted at home and abroad. Distributive capability denotes the equitable distribution of the resources obtained through extraction and regulation in society. The first three capabilities are directly related to the input function. In the "global village" environment, this aspect of the distribution of resources is more attractive for direct investments from abroad and the quantum of exports, which indicates the effectiveness of distributive capability and symbolic capability; likewise, it also exposes the integration of a state through symbols, monuments, slogans, words, and achievements. Meanwhile, responsive capability relates to the output function and demonstrates the system's response to the influx of demand from the public sector. This responsiveness has always been subject to the first four capabilities. If those capabilities are utilized promptly and effectively, the response to the incoming demands will be adequately positive.

The present debate on the ideal form of governance encompasses marinating an equilibrium between individual freedom and collective responsibility. All societies are constrained to deal with universal complexities, such as geopolitical turbulence, economic instability, technological disruption, social deprivations, economic inequalities, and environmental threats. Neither preconceived theories nor Western models provide the best-suited strategies to fulfill the demands above. However, adaptability seems to be an ideal choice so far.[17] It is only possible through effective leadership and efficient utilization of system capabilities.

The system's capabilities are essential for explaining the impact of globalization in any society as it is different from governance and its other forms. Governance is a way to run any system or government. It is always different in different countries, but system capabilities always exist in each society (democratic, monarchic, authoritative, dictatorial, fascist, or any other form) in the same form. It is leadership that utilizes its capabilities according to its vision and exposure. The efficiency level of these system capabilities determines any society's economic development and governance level. Governance may be good or bad, but system capabilities exist in any country. The usage of capabilities may be efficient or docile. Governance is concerned with resources and system capabilities are concerned with individuals and sources. Governance is dependent upon the efficiency of system capabilities. Therefore, to understand the impact of globalization in different domains, it is indispensable to understand the level of efficiency of system capability in China and India with their leadership qualities.

China and India are similar in a few ways; they are both densely populated emerging economies worldwide and extensive powers in Asia. They also have diversity like China is not prone to have a hegemony trend and always shows alienation towards world problems and does not allow any other power to poke its nose into her affairs. India allows the big powers, such as the US, to dismantle the balance of power in the region. – The Indian civil nuclear deal in 2008 did it. It (India) also has hegemonic designs, which is why it had problems with neighboring countries. India is the so-called largest democracy in the world, but China is a centrally controlled country under the guise of communism.

This treatise intends to be a comparative study that will measure the impact of globalization on the countries under discussion through the lens of leadership and its exploitation of system capabilities. It will also attempt to explain how China and India can affect the international environment in the age of globalization.

China and India are the two major powers in Asia. China is the second-largest economy[18] in the world, and India is the sixth-largest economy in the world[19] at the advent of the twenty-first century. China strives to surpass America's largest economy through its 'social capitalism' under communist ideology. For example, in 2015, the State Council suggested that equipment producers go global and characterized BRI implementation as "constructing an open new economic system." [20] China has the most significant exports in the world to America. On the other hand, India intends to be a regional and international player in economic, political, and cultural domains in a democratic framework.

A comparison between China and India divulges that external network strength varies between the two countries. Indian diasporas have got exposure ranging from New Delhi to Western International organizations (IOs) and MNCs. These professional diasporas have close ties to top national politicians and bureaucrats. However, they did not build strong ties with other local economic actors, such as parliament members and small-scale industrialists, considered prominent economic actors in India.

These lower-level economic actors served as a political force, and their opinion regarding liberalization was critical. Moreover, they expressed their opposing viewpoints on FDI liberalization through democratic channels. Because of the lack of ideational inflows, local economic actors viewed FDI and foreign goods as detrimental. On the other hand, the case of China is utterly different. FDI liberalization has been eased in China, as diasporas did not have strong ties at the top and provincial levels. Contrary to India, FDI liberalization quickly diffused in China due to the incorporation of the provincial government and local entrepreneurs.[21]

Globalization is a driving force; no individual or state can escape its effects. The countries that face the challenges of globalization and can adapt to the contemporary world keep flourishing. In contrast, countries with low-profile system capabilities cannot stand against this modern challenge (globalization). This economic divide makes a difference in the development of a country. Still, the fundamental indicators for developing a country are efficient system capabilities, adaptability, skilled social capital, high literacy, and good health and medical infrastructure.

In this age of globalization, China and India are two archetypal examples that are gaining advantages of globalization owing to their development above indicators. India is imperfect in its development indicators as its system capabilities are less effective than China's. Interestingly, although China is a communist regime, it has still taken advantage of globalization and has adopted the model of socialistic capitalism. While India is a so-called democratic state, it is also trying to get the fruits of globalization quite effectively.

China and India play an important role in determining Asia's policies. They are not belligerent against the apprehensions about globalization but face it pragmatically. They are enhancing their resources to face up to the competitive international environment. China became a member of the WTO in November 2001, and India is belatedly striving hard for its membership in the Association for the South East Asian Nations (ASEAN). Chinese membership in the WTO has increased the credibility of Chinese consumer products worldwide. She is excelling in low-tech, labor-intensive products and proving its dominance in technology domains.[22] Due to its exports, China is making swift headway in its economy and is considered to have the highest economic growth rate, which is 9 percent. Oded Shenkar underscores that China "… builds half of the world's microwave ovens, one-third of the television sets and air conditioners, a quarter of its washers and one-fifth of its refrigerators."[23] This growth rate will double until this book is published, and Chinese consumer and technological products will become more prevalent than ever before.

In 2014, Chinese President Xi Jinping declared while addressing Asian leaders in Shanghai, "It is for the people of Asia to run the affairs of Asia, solve the problems of Asia, and uphold the security of Asia." Although China's meteoric rise threatens its neighbors too, they are on the same page with China for not to be ruled by outsiders.[24] It shows that China is emerging as an economic giant in this century. It is conducting a dynamic foreign policy to play an essential role in the age of globalization. It intends to create a balance of power in the world dismantled by the U.S. after the disintegration of the Union of the Soviet Socialist Republic in December 1991.

The Belt and Road Initiative (BRI), launched in 2013, plays a significant role in attracting investors and increasing economic participation in the emerging markets of Eurasia. Furthermore, BRI encourages individual entrepreneurs; hence, it has succeeded in getting support from national agencies. Private manufacturers are not confined to typical BRI countries; instead, markets of underdeveloped BRI nations are targeted, too.[25]

Conversely, India is a mixed economy country, where system capabilities are in a state of abeyance. It (India) is a freewheeling society that always lives in the euphoria of being secular. The Indian political system is facing a paradoxical predicament as it is more democratic but less tolerant. It is not only less tolerant but also "less secular, less law-abiding, less liberal."[26] If India is illiberal, it means its democratic status is at stake. Since democracy and liberalism are intertwined. This is where China and India have a glaring difference as China holds up its system unleashed with social capitalism. At the same time, India, owing to its heterogeneous character, faces communal trends that circumvent India to play an active role in the modern world. Being an essential power in the region, India is facing disintegration at home owing to its intolerant attitude towards its communities.[27] Applying the same criterion in China seems more secular and tolerant than in India. Since 1949, hardly ever seen any other community in China remained under threat. It is officially atheist, Daoist (Taoist), and Buddhist. There are Han Chinese 91.9%, Zhuang, Uygur, Hui, Yi, Tibetan, Miao, Manchu, Mongol, Buyi, Korean, and other nationalities 8.1% (Christian 3%–4%, Muslim 1%–2%). Therefore, it is not as heterogeneous as India. Recently, in July 2009, the Muslim-majority province of Xinjiang, Urumqi, experienced severe ethnic riots. In India, examples of Hyderabad, Gujarat, and Ahmadabad are very pertinent, where Muslims were killed on a large scale and injured as well. Christians are also killed in India a few years back. Under Indra Gandhi, the Sikh community perished in India.

The communication revolution has compressed the world and intensified the consciousness of the world as a whole.[28] Therefore, India will no longer alienate itself from the world economy and has decided to open up its economy to the rest of the world.[29] The only problem India is facing today is pressure from some international actors and movements. For example, India is forced to sign the Comprehensive Test Ban Treaty under pressure from the U.S. In response, she will be unleashed to get permanent status in the Security Council of the United Nations. In the same way, India is also guilty in the domain of human rights violations in Gujarat, Hyderabad, and Kashmir. The West also pressurizes China to address its human rights violations and improve its relations with Taiwan, Tibet, and the Dalai Lama. Both countries are responding very well to the developed world as they have big, lucrative markets for the West.

It has been proved that Asia tends to grow even when the West lags. Numerous Western multinationals depend on Asia as it is a crucial growth driver due to high consumption levels. Economic roles are reversed now; Asia has been producing for the West in the past. Now, it's high time for the West to produce for Asia while focusing on job creation and simultaneously meeting the demands of hypercompetitive markets. Although the United States is not profoundly dependent on exports, 40 million jobs comprise exported goods. Asia also provides a fertile ground for the US workforce in the finance and technology sectors. Likewise, in China, Western markets have been opened to the Chinese middle class, but they have not succeeded because of data security. Latest surveys of Western business showed a significant shift in focus, including India, Pakistan, Indonesia, and the Philippines.[30]

The impact of globalization is varied as it is a relative phenomenon (it affects different things in a different environment in different ways). In China, the impact of globalization is different from that of India. Hence, this book will interpret some ground realities about the impact of globalization upon China and India in the twenty-first century, along with lessons for the third world that can be learned from the experience of these two major powers in Asia.

Besides, this tome construes that the theories of liberalism (free trade for mutual benefit by avoiding war) and mercantilism (economic nationalism) can be seen in the operational form in India. Marxism, neo-mercantilism (more exports and fewer imports), and liberalism, in the case of China, also remain intact. India believes in socio-political and economic development with the principles of free trade. It also believes in military might for its hegemonic tendency in the region. Depending upon the military, it might denote India's inclination towards mercantilism. On the other hand, we also found economic nationalism with more exports than imports in India, which transforms its economic system into neo-mercantilism. For sustainability in the international environment, it also follows liberal economic trends and permits foreign goods into its country. Therefore, interestingly, all theories of international political economy overlap each other in this document. It gives a categorical expression that this globalized world can be seen through the prism of theories in international relations. Still, being very complex in its (international environment) nature, most countries are run by liberalism with mercantilism. Here, we can call this 'liberacantilism.'[31] A theory that runs in most of the contemporary world under its strong influence.

Globalization and interdependence are different. Globalization is a unified process that believes in integrating political, economic, and social actors with non-state actors for the welfare of the whole.

Interdependence is a mechanism for conducting relations between two or more countries based on mutual understanding. It is more among states; globalization works at the macro level, while interdependence works at the micro level. In globalization, all political and nonpolitical actors work together across boundaries where the liberal and private sectors look more active. Interdependence is usually based on relations among nations; individuals hardly ever come into contact, but in globalization, the individual is the unit of the whole process.

The book's last chapter explains how the countries under discussion make a difference while efficiently managing the COVID-19 pandemic, and leaders exploit their system capabilities with a clear difference.

Endnotes

1 Parag Khanna, *THE FUTURE IS ASIAN: Commerce, Conflict, and Culture in the 21st Century*: Simon & Schuster, 2019,22.

2 James H. Mittelman, *Globalization Syndrome: Transformation and Resistance,* New Jersey: Princeton University press, 2000, 04.

3 Ibid.

4 Terms like "democratization of technology," "democratization of finance," and "democratization of information" have been used by Thomas L. Friedman, *Understanding Globalization: The Lexus and the Olive Tree*, New York: Anchor Books, Inc., 1999, 46-72.

5 Anthony Giddens, *The Consequences of Modernity,* Cambridge: Polity Press, 1990, 64 cited in James H. Mittelman, *Globalization Syndrome*, 06.

6 Benjamin R. Barber, *Jihad Vs. McWorld,* New York: Ballantine Books Inc., 1996. Alien culture Macs means, MTV, McDonalds, and Macintosh, has no conformity with the home cultural heritage. For instance, the food restaurants are full of young guys and girls wearing trousers and shirts alike. It has become very difficult to recognize a boy or girl by their external appearance. A long ponytail can be seen borne by young boys. In traditional societies like China and India, some Fast-food restaurants have dance clubs where boys do not hesitate to dance with their partners. This is all due to these MNCs and the communication revolution. The wiring of the world has inter-connected the people so that it has become impossible to recognize whether one is sitting in China, India, America, or Europe.

7 Parag Khanna, *THE FUTURE IS ASIAN: Commerce, Conflict, and Culture in the 21st Century*: Simon & Schuster, 2019,9.

8 Min Ye, *The Belt Road, and Beyond: State-Mobilized Globalization in China: 1998-2018*: Cambridge University Press, 2020,193.

9 Min Ye, *Diasporas and Foreign Direct Investment in China and India*: Cambridge University Press, 2014, 144-145.

10 Parag Khanna, *THE FUTURE IS ASIAN: Commerce, Conflict, and Culture in the 21st Century*: Simon & Schuster, 2019,10-12.

11 Gabriel A. Almond and G. Bingham Powell Jr., *Comparative Politics: A developmental Approach,* Boston: Little, Brown and Company INC., 1966, pp. 190-212.

12 Min Ye, *Diasporas and Foreign Direct Investment in China and India*: Cambridge University Press, 2014, 03.

13 Kenichi Ohmae, *The End of Nation States: The Rise of Regional Economies,* New York: Simon and Schuster Inc., 1996, 02-3.

14 Parag Khanna, *THE FUTURE IS ASIAN: Commerce, Conflict, and Culture in the 21st Century*: Simon & Schuster, 2019,258.

15 Migration of dreams and relative deprivation are used by Richard J. Payne and Jamal R. Nassar, *Politics and Cultures in the Developing World: The Impact of Globalization,* New York: Priscilla McGeehon, 2003, 115.

16 Almond and Powell, *Comparative Politics*, 190-212.

17 Parag Khanna, *THE FUTURE IS ASIAN: Commerce, Conflict, and Culture in the 21st Century*: Simon & Schuster, 2019,255.

18 Oded Shenkar, *The Chinese Century: The Rising Chinese Economy and Its Impact on the Global Economy, the Balance of Power, and Your Job*, Wharton School Publishing, University of Pennsylvania, 2005, 02.

19 Rajen Harshe, "The Challenges of Globalization" in B. Ramesh Babu (ed.), *Globalization and the South Asian State*, Denver, Colorado: International Academic Publishers, 1998, 28.

20 Min Ye, *The Belt Road, and Beyond: State-Mobilized Globalization in China: 1998-2018*: Cambridge University Press, 2020,134.

21 Min Ye, *Diasporas and Foreign Direct Investment in China and India*: Cambridge University Press, 2014,88.

22 Oded Shenkar, *The Chinese Century*, 2-3.

23 Ibid.

24 Parag Khanna, *THE FUTURE IS ASIAN: Commerce, Conflict, and Culture in the 21st Century*, Simon & Schuster, 2019, 15.

25 Min Ye, *The Belt Road, and Beyond: State-Mobilized Globalization in China: 1998-2018*: Cambridge University Press, 2020,165.

26 Fareed Zakaria, *The Future of Freedom: Illiberal democracy at Home and Abroad*, New York: W.W. Norton Co., 2004, 106.

27 Rajen Harshe, "The Challenges of Globalization," 30.

28 Ibid., 19.

29 Ibid., 28.

30 Parag Khanna, *The Future is Asian: Commerce, Conflict, and Culture in the 21st Century*: Simon & Schuster, 2019,191-192.

31 Liberacantilism (a mixture of liberalism and mercantilism) means that the contemporary world usually intermixes different concepts to adjust to the international environment. China is restructuring and reviewing its economic system but not its political system. Therefore, it adopts economic nationalism and mercantilism and believes in free trade with certain implications, calling it liberalism. That impurity or amalgam of different concepts makes the modern world system more complex.

Chapter I. Globalization: A Historical Perspective

Political scientists argue that globalization started with the Treaty of Westphalia in 1648. In ancient times, people lived together in the form of families, tribes, villages, and city-states. The nature of increased interconnectedness was different. It was not as fast and dynamic as today due to technological and communication revolutions.

Modern globalization may be considered a phenomenon that intends to create a global village. It is considered that why a global village, why not a world government or a world city or a global city. As we know, the word 'village' gives an understanding that it is where most people live together and are usually very close.

The North uses new methods to attract the South for its vital interests. After the First World War in 1918, the market economy was prevalent, and after the Second World War in 1945, the drums of democracy were beaten heavily. In the wake of the disintegration of the former Soviet Union in 1991, the North always used NWO, Global Village, Human Rights, Governance, and Sustainable Human Development for its ax to grind. Economic gains and profit maximization had been the main agenda of the economic cartels in the past. In this modern era, Multinational Corporations (MNCs) are run by the same old economic cartels ruling over the world. International Financial Institutions (IFIs) are underpinning these MNCs. The MNCs have transformed into Multinational Governments (MNGs) or Multinational States (MNS) with all their resources and technological sophistication that have the strings in their hands. In the contemporary world, economic resources are limited, but competitors are more. Therefore, competition has increased insecurity in the world.

Furthermore, the world experienced a relatively stable Western order as the tussle to conquer one another stopped after World War Two. Globalization of politics prevailed in the form of international alliances and institutions such as the North Atlantic Treaty Organization (NATO), the United Nations, the World Bank, and the International Monetary Fund (IMF). Seventy years back, the functionality of these international bodies and agreements was not scrupulously contemplated; however, with the end of the Cold War, Western liberalism, democracy, and capitalism triumphed. The period in the 1990s was vital in transforming the world order into a purely globalized order as numerous former Soviet republics became members of the European Union and NATO. Besides these republics, many developing countries joined the World Trade Organization (WTO). Eventually, the Washington Consensus introduced the world to the ideas of an integrated economy through free trade, economic deregulation, the Western economic system, flows of capital, and culture to set the global agenda.[1]

The Communication Revolution, IFIs, advertisements, aggressive marketing, and, above all, the MNGs have put an end to the traditional form of the state that used to be based on four essential elements: Sovereignty, Government, Territory, and Population. The MNGs are dictating the modern states owing to their economic power. Besides that, weapons of mass destruction (WMD) and missile races in different parts of the world have also diminished the very concept of the state or its well-defined boundaries and given way to these MNGs. The modern state has to redefine its character; otherwise, the MNGs will take it under its sway with all its technological sophistication and scientific advancements.

It seems likely that the modern state is facing a crisis of selective morality (something is suitable for the few and wrong for the rest of the world. As the atomic bomb is suitable for the big powers, Israel and India, but wrong for Iran, North Korea, Pakistan, and others) under the umbrella of so-called interdependence, democracy, environmental pollution, weapons of mass destruction, violation of human rights and terrorism. Due to the selective behavior of the political and nonpolitical elite, the state system has shattered into pieces. The incident of 9/11 in 2001, a pertinent example in this context, exposes the feeble meanings of modern globalization. The meanings of state sovereignty, government, territory, and population have changed altogether. If the state is sovereign internally and externally, how was it attacked by an individual sitting or residing in Afghanistan (as blamed by the U.S. government), and America retaliated with cruise missiles of one million dollars apiece?[2] Osama Bin Laden is not a state but an individual who waged war against the sole superpower of the world. It means in this communication age, an individual can assume the status of a state, or there is an end of the state as an institution.

America invaded Iraq in 1991 to knock it out of Kuwait and Afghanistan in 2001 and again Iraq in 2003 in the name of restoring human rights and democracy. Strangely, democracy and human rights are being restored with a military invasion. If the military could do so, why the melting pot (America) opposes military rule in Pakistan and other developing countries? Why are economic and political sanctions imposed in countries with military rules instead of democracy? From 1895 to 2003, America invaded different countries in Asia, Latin America, and Africa more or less 18 times and did its best to install democracy in those countries but remained unsuccessful. Therefore, it looks like, before the Second World War, Colonialism jeopardized the nation-state that sowed the seeds of nationalism among people. The present-day world is a victim of neo-colonialism, which is an indirect control of the North to the South through economic, political, and social means. The rising tide of the communication stronghold tells us the truth about the abduction of the world by the hands of the MNGs.

The Europeanization and Americanization of the nineteenth and twentieth centuries influenced many nations in numerous ways: European administration, U.S. military intervention, currency in the form of U.S. dollar dominance of American social media., and so forth. Billions of people are personally or psychologically connected to the West through language, sports, Hollywood, and social media.[3]

If we look at the origin of globalization, the following chronological evolution of globalization can be observed. The individual is the unit of this process as a cell of the human body. The apogee of globalization is terrorism, which is a sheer result of relative deprivation. Monopolizing resources by the industrialized world during the two World Wars of the twentieth century kept the dependency theory (a hypothetical claim that the North had developed itself at the expense of the South) in an action that ultimately depleted the South and repleted the North.

GLOBALIZATION CHRONOLOGICAL EVOLUTION

INDIVIDUAL
FAMILY
TRIBES
VILLAGES
CITY-STATES
STATES
EMPIRES
MERCANTALISM
NEOMERCANTALISM
COLONIALISM
MONOPOLIZATION BY THE HAVES
TWO WORLD WARS (1914-18, 1939-45)
DEMOCRACY
NATIONAL LIBERATION
NEOCOLONIALISM
ELECTRONIC COLONIALISM
EMERGENCE OF MULTINATIONAL CORPORATIONS
INTERNATIONAL FINANCIAL INSTITUTIONS
NEOLIBERALISM
FREE MARKET
DEPRIVATION AMONG THE LOCAL GROUPS
GLOBALIZATION
RISE OF REGIONALISM
TERRORISM

Here, the digital divide starts and creates an everlasting lacuna between 'haves' and 'have-nots.' With all its technological and scientific advancements, the West wayed the whole developing world's resources. It made them realize their lack of resources through communication and media that, consequently, wage war against the West and the rest. The previous chronology shows the evolutionary process of globalization and how it started historically. Therefore, it evolved into an evolutionary process that profoundly impacted the modern world. This chronological order aims to introduce the reader to how (globalization) emerged in the world.

The above-mentioned chronological order explains that globalization is a gradual process that starts with an individual's birth. Steadily, it transforms itself in different forms and levels. In the classical state system, globalization was not as fast as today. The scientific and technological developments of the twentieth century have revolutionized the phenomenon of globalization. It sped it up, compressed space and time, and left the developing world on vacation. The developed world copes with the ongoing rush of globalization and updates itself accordingly. This causes a digital divide between the West and the rest. It gave rise to regionalism; the countries with effective system capabilities enjoyed the change, such as the European Union, as a success story. Contrary to this, the South Asian Association for Regional Cooperation, the Organization of African Countries, the Organization of Islamic Conference, and the North American Free Trade Agreement are not success stories. It resulted in deprivation and provoked terrorism that annihilated the world relentlessly.

Globalization: Theoretical Perspective

People wish to live together under one government in one universal world. This is what globalization means in the modern world. In this world where few can go anywhere, the rest face visa constraints and immigration problems. This is a pertinent question for the proponents of globalization in the modern world who believe in neoliberalism (end of state control of the economy), free-market, laissez-faire, democracy, and universal peace.

The free-market economy has become a passion for the developed world today; James H. Mittelman says: "Today, competitiveness, or free-market competition, has been elevated to an ideology, and this icon represents an important element in the globalization matrix."[4] Richard D'Aveni calls it "hyper-competition" or an intensive endeavor to augment market volatility and institute business improbability.[5]

State-mobilized globalization is based on two primary mechanisms. The first suggests utilizing the tool of political mobilization to promote active and unrestricted growth, hence stimulating globalization processes. The second one refers to the incorporation of intrastate fragmentation that constrains political intervention to mobilize state agencies and lower-level units to accelerate globalization. [6]

Internet, cyberspace, email, and fax machines are such tools in the hands of an individual living in the 21st century, who can exploit such tools or resources for his political, economic, social, or any other benefit. Private TV channels through cable networks are available in most countries. These channels are commercial; anyone can buy time to communicate their message. Advertisements are so fascinating that giant MNGs have curtailed the area of choice for the clients. Marketing has become so aggressive that hardly one can escape from buying anything. Credit cards help people become subject to creditors.

Coca-Cola, Compaq, Dell, Fahrenheit, Ford, General Motors, IBM, KFC, Marlboro, Macintosh, McDonald's, Mercedez Benz, Nike, Pepsi, Pizza Hutt, Vitech, etc. are such Multinational corporations (MNCs) that have become mini-states or mini governments within countries like Bangladesh, Canada, China, India, Japan, Pakistan, UK, U.S.A., etc. The MNGs are ruling over the world.

Monopolization of capital is the main objective of these MNGs. This monopolization is not new for the nation-states. In the sixteenth and seventeenth centuries, imperialist states such as Great Britain, Portugal, Hungary, Germany, and Italy acted similarly. In the eighteenth and nineteenth centuries, colonial powers, including all imperial powers, and the New World (the U.S.) followed suit. Subsequently, after World War II (1945), a period of neocolonialism started- dependency theory (the theory calls for monopolizing the resources of the satellite states by the colonial powers) underscores that monopolized the world economic resources. In the past, states usually monopolized resources, but in modern times, individuals or groups of individuals did so with profit maximization.

The democratization of information through the Internet, the democratization of finance through credit cards, and the democratization of technology through computers[7] have made the end of the state. Francis Fukuyama's End of History is utterly at stake; modern man does not enjoy the freedom of constitutional liberalism.

Nevertheless, the factual position is that the MNGs of America and Japan are leading contestants. The former tends to capture the world through its McWorld, the latter through its technology. Benjamin R. Barber's McWorld is a Macintosh, MTV, and McDonald's collection that believes in the commercial revolution. McWorld controls information, communication, and entertainment and will eventually control human destiny. It also mesmerizes people with fast music, computers, and fast food through MTV, Macintosh, and McDonald's.[8]

Southeast Asia is considered the only postcolonial region that adopted cross-border intergradation and steadiness, similar to the early times of the European Union. The population of approximately 700 million is religiously, culturally, and ethnically diverse. The Association of Southeast Asian Nations (ASEAN) comprises Indian, Chinese, Arabian, and European immigrants. Religious rituals of millions of Muslims, Christians, Buddhists, and Hindus are widespread in the region. Transborder linkages are preserved because of family businesses like the bamboo network of Chinese ethnicity and the network of Muslims. Beyond India, China, Japan, and Australia, the region developed global linkages to the Gulf countries, Europe, the U.S., and Latin America.[9]

Kenichi Ohmae talks about the borderless world in his latest document, The End of the Nation-State: The Rise of Regional Economies, published in 1996. This book assists in arguing that globalization deprives the modern state of sovereignty and government in an absolute sense.

He describes four "Is" (Investment, Industry, Information Technology, and Individual) as a 'sine qua non for economic development.[10] The close study of his thoughts exposes the reality of the developed world flush with surplus cash for investment. Japan is a country that has more than 10 trillion U.S. $ and intends to invest in the world to get a massive profit out of it. America has the same tendency to invest or export its surplus to gain an advantage. It gives a real boost to the economies of such countries. Sometimes, a country is near bankruptcy but has a tremendous amount of cash in the form of pension funds and life insurance, and such cash has no profit in the same geographical area. So, such countries invest the same cash in other countries to get profit from that public money.

The American government is investing 10 percent of pension funds in Asia and getting a tremendous interest rate. So, the investment is not constrained by geographical boundaries; investors invest their money wherever the opportunity is. Investment comes not only from the public sector but also from the public sector. Ten years ago, most of the time, "the flow of cross border funds was primarily from the government to government or from multilateral lending agency to government."[11] With the advent of economic globalization, the flow of cross-border funds is now private, and the government hesitates to be involved at either end. Mostly, this investment is done through MNCs.

Atul Kohli (2004,382) uses the metaphor of liability to define foreign capital as FDI contributes to weakening a state's autonomy. Contrary to that, some globalists appreciate the integration of China's industrialization with MNCs. However, it is essential to notice that nearly all debates and writings on FDI categorize this capital as flowing from the West.[12]

It means these giant MNCs have transformed into MNGs or MNS. These newly economically sound MNGs or MNS have their subjects, government, and sovereignty but no territory, as they believe in a borderless world. For example, in Pakistan, McDonald's, KFC, and Pizza Hut are fast-food restaurants where people feel more comfortable with their paramours even though police cannot check them in the vicinity of these restaurants. This freedom attracts the Pakistani young generation more as they feel insecure at any other public place in the country. The same is the case in India; therefore, these MNG's rulings over such generations are their subjects. As the local police are not concerned with their free environment, they (MNGs) are sovereign and independent in their small vicinity. These MNGs have complete control over developing countries' economies and are very strong in the developed world.

John Kenneth's analysis categorically stresses that giant corporations (MNGs) dominate the U.S. economy. Their strategic influence on economic and political affairs and the imperative need of their corporations for their safety and protection to control their sources of raw materials and their markets.

Let's look at the past few decades. It lets us know. Looking back to the past half-century tells us that the main objective of the United States military encroachment into the Arab world was to preclude oil flow, mainly to the United States and Europe. Historically, the same resource has been used as a weapon against the West. For example, during the Yom Kippur War, the oil prices were pushed up five-fold by Gulf exporters. However, despite increasing self-sufficiency, Europe and the United States have been minimizing their dependency on Gulf energy. Gradually, the United States' priorities shifted towards increasing arms sales to Gulf countries, the sociopolitical stability of Iraq, and containing the new regime of Iran. The unanswered efforts of the United States to transform the Gulf Cooperation Council into NATO of an already devastating region left the United States disappointed.[13]

The cumulative effect of the annual flow of investment results in an economic involvement much greater than exports. So, U.S. foreign policy is mainly based on controlling the globe directly or indirectly with an energetic expansionist policy of U.S. business. The industry is the second "I" that boosts the modern phenomenon of globalization. Now, under economic globalization, MNGs have come into action. They usually manufacture the people's desires through advertisements and marketing to attract the people of the world. Therefore, people have started demanding the local market to bring their desired products. In this way, it becomes an inability for the trader to bring foreign products to satisfy their demands.

GM, IBM, P&G, and Unilever are MNGs in China working successfully and comfortably to expand their business. Third, "I" is information technology, which has created a global village, and the whole world has come under its sway without any hindrance. Investment and industry are being facilitated by information technology. It kept them moving and alive. Electronic commerce is a product of information technology. "Which now makes it possible for a company to operate in various parts of the world without building up an entire business system in each country where it has a presence."[14]

The wiring of the world of the Internet has made it possible for any individual, whether he is an engineer, designer, architect, planner, scientist, or sociologist, to control his business abroad. The individual consumer is the fourth "I" who compels the market to bring the best and cheapest product, no matter where it comes from.

By the mid-1990s, local officials in eastern China observed that Western MNCs and diasporas played a significant role in bringing prosperity. These local officials became more interested in FDI liberalization. [15] The MNGs with developed resources can easily compete in the world market by choosing the policy of dumping (A term used in economics that means selling off products below their production cost to capture the market against rival companies) at the outset. In the modern global economy, the nature and size of business units matter in developing a country.[16] The nation-states have borders and connections that are considered in the borderless world.[17]

Information technology seems to have transformed the whole universe altogether, and it has become quite challenging to understand the reality of any product on the market. They want to develop a world where they could monopolize the capital. Lenin rightly said that capitalist countries always have "The urgency to develop a world market, the struggle to control foreign sources of raw materials, the competitive hunt for the colonies, and the tendency towards the concentration of capital."[18]

These MNGs are working on multiplying playing a drama in which every character tries to get an Oscar through its excellent performance without knowing the element of selective morality on the part of the jury. The UN, being a so-called central authority, has failed to a certain extent to check the ongoing race of McDonaldization of the world.

This jungle-like world is whole of ethnic identities fighting with each other, for example, Kurds in Iraq, rival groups in Afghanistan, Quebec in Canada, Tamil in Sri Lanka, Serbians and Croats in the former Yugoslavia, etc., so it is tough for the modern state to unify them. Still, these MNGs are integrating them well through their taste, advertisements, slogans, and environment.

Barber exposes that McWorld believes in extreme commercialism. It sometimes disguises itself under the name of democracy and gets hold of predacious markets.[19] Contrary to this, multiculturalism turned into a malignant tumor, kept dividing sovereign identities, and could not serve to sustain the modern sovereign state system's success.[20] Markets in the world dislike frontiers as nature dislikes a vacuum. Here, Benjamin R. Barber testifies to Kenichi Ohmae's borderless world.

"Within their expensive and permeable domains, interests are private, trade is free, currencies are convertible, access to banking is open, contracts are enforceable (the state's legitimate economic function), and the laws of productions and consumption are sovereign, trumping the laws of legislatures and courts."[21]

In Europe, Asia, and America, International Financial Institutions, trade organizations, transnational lobbies like OPEC, international news agencies like CNN, BBC, and Zee News, and MNGs are busy reshaping the world through their activities.[22] Sometimes, products are made in any one of the following countries: China, Korea, Hong Kong, Malaysia, Singapore, Taiwan, Mauritius, Thailand, Indonesia, Mexico, and the Philippines, but it becomes difficult to trace the origin of any product.[23] Gillette's chairman, Alfred M. Zeien, says firmly that I do not find any foreign country in business, but I used to modify the products to any marketplace.[24]

The MNGs, which can also be remembered as transnational, post-national, and antinational, have become central players in the Global Economy. They have left behind the sovereign state and represent peoplehood.[25]

"Their customers are not a citizen of a particular nation or members of parochial clan: they belong to the universal tribe of consumers defined by needs and wants that are ubiquitous, if not by nature than by the cunning of advertising."[26]

McWorld serves 20 million customers worldwide every day and attracts more and more people daily. People are using McWorld products from all over the world; Reebok shoes, Fahrenheit perfumes, Safari, and Ralph Lauren have ended the frontiers of the world.[27]

In 1992, the number one fast-food restaurant in Japan, considered by volume of customers, was McDonald's, and Colonel's Kentucky Fried Chicken got the number two position.[28] It shows how California-ization has influenced the Japanese. Kenichi Ohmae says the convergence process of taste and preference is called California-ization.[29] All these developments slit open three broad effects of MNGs' economic policy:

I.   They can transfer capital anywhere in the world.
II. Company men have been made more responsive, taking care of customers' demands and fulfilling them accordingly.
III. Economic nationalization can hardly influence the purchase decision in the prevailing conditions, as acculturation has become a state symbol in developing countries.[30]

The middle-class urbanized consumers of Asia are the main attraction for Western retailers. However, Western brands fail to salivate the 400 millennials to the extent their parents are attracted. The present trend shows that Asians are more likely to purchase Asian goods in comparison to those manufactured by the West. For example, billions of Southeast Asians purchase refrigerators from Godrej, LG, and Haier.[31]

The MNGs abhor government intervention in the market's decision-making process. The developed countries intend to squeeze the last drop of blood from the frail sovereign entities of the developing world.[32] That is why the developed world is busy maximizing its sales and holding the economic markets in a capitalist fashion. Whenever sovereign entities want to attract their (MNGs) attention toward state-generated public interests like justice, full employment, and environmental protection, the MNGs feel it is against their interests. They decide to withdraw their investments from that country without giving prior notice and by leaving indigenous employees in the lurch, even without giving them compensatory amounts.

This is by the natural philosophy of laissez-faire, "Leave us alone! Let us do what producers and consumers do: Sell, Buy, Produce, Consume."[33] Barber calls laissez-faire a force with a new label of McWorld, based on internationalism and global markets. This kind of laissez-faire of the capitalist 'haves' can also be adequate to the Marxian concept of an economic war between the rich and the poor countries.[34] It can also be translated in Hobbes Levi Athenian's approach as a "War of all against all… the quest for power after power that ceaseth only in death."[35]

International Financial Institutions

International Financial Institutions (IFIs) are another source of MNGs to rule over the world and put an end to the state. The IMF and the WB work as guarantors of the U.S. while giving economic aid and loans to developing nations. The World Bank tries to redress the grievances of the developing world through its welfare schemes and programs. The presidency of James Wolfenson commenced in 1995 with the primary objective of alleviating poverty in civil society in the developing world. The bank also intended to reduce the debt burdens of highly indebted poor countries (HIPC).

The critics think that the WB acts as little but speaks much. All these reforms have been a direct result of the 'Washington consensus' in which some structural adjustments and economic liberalization measures were imposed in 1980 and 1990 to make reforms in the macroeconomic policies of under-developed countries. Contrary to this, IMF has confined it to reform, releasing information, and facilitating its national and international oversight systems.[36]

The IMF has proposed, "A broader range of institutional reforms is needed if countries are to establish and maintain private sector confidence and thereby lay the basis for sustained growth."[37] It has confined itself and restrained to specific issues like institutional reforms of the treasury, budget preparation and approval procedures, tax administering, accounting and audit procedures, Central Bank Operations, and official statistics functions. As far as market mechanism is concerned, it deals with exchange, trade, price systems, and aspects of the financial systems. In regulatory and legal affairs, (IMF) concentrates on taxation, banking sector laws and regulations, and establishing free and fair market entry.[38] The IMF authorities claim that they keep the secrecy and centralization of power.

During the East Asian crisis in the late 1990s, the concerned government called them 'poorly supervised,' 'poorly functioning,' 'badly regulated,' 'corrupt,' and 'government-directed.'[39]

The IMF does not consider the IFIs responsible for the East Asian crisis. Such a statement showed a reversal in IMF's policy when they used to call the same countries 'tigers,' economic 'miracles,' and 'impressive' etc.[40] A few years later, the IMF accepted that it had some connections to those crises.[41] The IFIs' transparency and accountability are deficient; a protest was made in Washington to condemn the WB and the IMF.[42]

The above description shows that the IFIs are the puppets in the hands of the developed world. America utilizes a network of banks, corporations, restaurants, and other consumer goods. Coca-Cola, Hershey, KFC, Levi's, Marlboro, McDonald's, Nike, Pepsi, and Wrigley all serve the American purpose and achieve their profit motive in the far-flung areas of the world in their unique style and fashion, attracting every generation.[43]

The MNGs are busy in economic pursuits, employing their industry, arms, food, music, fashion, films, and culture. American culture is an amalgam of different communities worldwide. It has become a melting pot where hundreds live in a good knitting unit. Capitalist ideology keeps everyone united by fulfilling their needs and demands in time. The government employs internal integrity and peace abroad to rule over the world.

American consumer goods are hardly American by origin but are known as American goods. For example, Chevy is a famous automobile in America built in Mexico with imported parts and then reimported into the U.S. The same case is with Ford, which was built in Germany by Turkish workers and sold in Hong Kong and Nigerian markets.[44] Economic globalization is against the essence of Ricardo's theory of Comparative Advantage. In economic globalization, the advantage lies purely in the developed world.[45] The modern state has become a satellite of the MNGs and the World Trade Organization (WTO).

World Trade Organization

Another multilateral international institution is also active in conducting trade between nations. The WTO came into existence on January 1, 1995. Almost all the trading nations, including Pakistan, are members of the WTO. This international body has three main objectives:

I. To keep the trade flow smooth.
II. To assist as a medium for trade negotiations.
III. To settle disputes among states in trade affairs.

All member nations know the rules and regulations of conducting trade through WTO. Its rules are transparent and predictable. The trading nations trade confidently because all the agreements and contracts are signed after considerable debate and controversy. The WTO also assists developing countries in the affairs of technical know-how and trains them accordingly. In 1999, China's Trade Minister, Long Yongtu, gave a detailed interview emphasizing that China aims to extract economic benefits and increase political influence worldwide by joining the WTO.[46] Contrary to this, Bretton Woods institutions are only working for the MNGs of the world, especially for American MNGs. In this way, these MNGs are depleting the world's resources unilaterally.

This is where a sense of deprivation starts, especially in the developing world. This deprivation is leading the world towards terrorism, and unfortunately, it is being faced by the state, not by the MNGs. The MNGs finish off their business from the country where terrorist activities become a routine matter and start business in peaceful countries. It lessens the profit margin because, in the third world, MNGs earn more than in the developed world. These MNGs are running after profit maximization without considering the welfare of the whole.

The question that arises here is why MNGs emerge as rulers instead of the state. After the Second World War in 1945, nation-states started manufacturing weapons of mass destruction, and an arms race started between rival states. This arms race also encompassed the developing world. Contrary to this, the MNGs are inclined towards peace and entertaining people with music, computers, and fast food.

The communication revolution assisted business people's motive of profit maximization. Now, multimedia has exaggerated things so fast that whatever is said in media is considered valid. False news of scientific and technological advancement is spread through the media to influence the public. For example, it was popularized in the late 1990s that America had made a stealth plane that was very advanced and could detect any covert plans going on in the world during its flight. It was exaggerated as this plane could detect even what was being cooked in the cattle of any home. If it was so, why could America not detect that the World Trade Center and the Pentagon were going to be attacked on September 11, 2001? Why America could not see that Pakistan had made a Nuclear Bomb? Why could America not find out about nuclear deals done by European and

Asian Scientists?

One day, this exaggeration will take the form of any private channel announcing that God is online, the host saying hello to God, and then banging everything will set fire. The host remained unharmed and told his boss that God was online, and when I started talking, everything set ablaze. The BBC may explain this as God was online in such a country when the host said hello to God, and as He (God) responded, everything set ablaze as God's sound frequency was more significant than the average sound frequency.

CNN likely explains this event that does not worry about God's Sound frequency; our men are at work at Mercury and trying to get in contact with God - they will fix everything right very soon; consequently, communication revolution and MNGs are going hand in hand and exploiting the state resources for their purpose.

Indubitably, Asia is at the core of global industrial output. Still, automation seems to have become a more serious threat to employment than the tariffs imposed by the U.S. or outsourcing to America and Europe. Automation is not confined to the West but is equally unfolding in Asia. Besides the sorting robots of Amazon and Alibaba, Universal robots (UR) contribute to the double-digit annual growth of Asia. However, the Asian expanding sectors vary from those of the West, where customers' shift to Amazon leaves the shopping malls empty, and Facebook and Google crush print newspapers. Despite swelling e-commerce in Asia, shopping malls are packed, news presses continue churning, and physical and digital demands for everything persistently rise.[47]

Thomas L. Friedman considers the idea of the end of the state as nonsense.[48] But he writes on the same page, "In the Cold War, the size of the state mattered. You needed the big state to fight the communists, maintain the walls around your country, and sustain a generous welfare system to buy off your workers so they wouldn't go communist. In the era of globalization (rule of MNGs), the quality of the state matters."[49]

Now, people are more quality-conscious. They can spend money on quality products. Friedman admits that the size of the state is not considered, but the quality matters of a product that is only being given by the MNGs. He again says, "The electronic herd turns the whole world into a parliamentary system, in which every government lives under the fear of a no-confidence vote from the herd."[50]

He calls electronic herds to the private sector run directly by MNGs. He called MNGs longhorn cattle. The facts and figures show how these MNGs control the world's economic output. According to the WB report, in 1970, the local factories that are associated with the MNGs earned 4.5% of the world's Gross Domestic Product (GDP). The earnings of the MNGs have doubled today.[51] In 1987, MNGs' direct investment in the developing world accounted for 0.4 %of their total GDP and has increased by more than 2%.[52]

It is happening not only in the developing world but worldwide. When discussing his Golden Straitjacket, free-market capitalism, he emphatically argues, "Which system today is the most effective at generating rising living standards? The historical debate is over. The answer is free-market capitalism."[53]

This is how we can derive that free-market capitalism is the economic policy of the MNGs. They know this is the only way to satisfy the demands of the present generation. It is against the modern concept of sustainable human development (SHD) as it (SHD) fulfills the demands and needs of the present generations without compromising upon the needs of future generations.

We are pleased with their economic designs but do not agree with their actions based on selective morality and profit maximization at the cost of future generations. If these MNGs are serious about having a universal market, they must be more pragmatic in their policies and actions. For example, the visa policy for third-world countries is highly biased. People cannot go to the world to find their life prospects independently.

Contrary to this, these MNGs are a brain drain in the world and give jobs to extraordinary people in information technology, science, and engineering. The MNGs pay them high perks and allure them towards their bright future. It deprives the nation-states of such brilliant and talented social capital.

The MNGs are not a nuisance; their multinational states concept is very close to human nature and keeps more people dynamic and united. It can help minimize the digital divide between the North and the South. But pragmatism is missing, which is why terrorism is in action. A sense of deprivation among the many and satisfaction among the few will likely destroy this planet.

Samuel P. Huntington's thesis of the clash of civilizations will come true, which will be a real misfortune for the world. The 9/11 incident admonishes us and warns MNGs to be practical and give everybody's share according to one's capabilities and talent. Profit maximization may transform into terror maximization. May God forbid us and keep this world peaceful and prosperous.

The MNGs are creating a revolution silently but rapidly. We may call it a *covert revolution* that is not beyond anyone but very close to everyone, and anyone is unaware of it. Thanks to the communication revolution, it is impossible to escape from it. If the supporters of nation-states wish to carry on the modern state system, they must adopt a hardheaded approach to maintain it. They need to assure the sovereignty and integrity of the state in a true sense. Examples of Iraq, Afghanistan, Kashmir, Palestine, and Israel are before us, where the state is helpless in performing its affairs. Afghanistan and Iraq are pertinent and classical examples in this backdrop where the American administration is working.

This selective morality perhaps will not sow the seeds of increased interconnectedness properly so that the West could harvest a crop of globalization. It does not mean we should blame America or the developed world for our weaknesses. It is wrong and misperception. It is quite natural, for instance, that an individual with more resources constantly regulates the affairs in his way- if any other person of his status appears, he gives way to him for a better understanding of each other. If the newcomer is more influential, he quickly sets aside the first. The first automatically shows allegiance towards him without any resistance. The modern state is like an individual. The more resourceful states are ruling over the world, and the states with fewer resources have to live with their few resources without depending upon the resources. The states that depend on other resourceful states must become slaves of their masters (resourceful). So, to be dictated to by their masters is the fate of the enslaved people. In this age of globalization, we can see a digital divide between the South and the North. From the perspective of the above discussion, we can have a division of states as follows:

Masters-Moderators-Slaves

Masters include America, Britain, Canada, France, Germany, and Italy; moderators include China, Russia, Brazil, Australia, Portugal, and Israel. Slave states include all developing countries of Asia, Africa, and Latin America. India has a unique status in the community of nations. Its size, population, and system capabilities make it neither an enslaver nor an enslaved person. Its status as a moderator is also taking the limelight due to its unstable political and economic system. So, in such a complex communication-ridden world, it has become challenging for governments to conceal facts from any sane person.

Globalization is not a curse, but it is only advantageous for those who have done the homework. It is evident in the international political order that the power of adaptability is the sine qua non for a stable political system. Intense globalization processes have marked the past two decades, and China has adapted to the challenges of globalization either by the expectation of convergence or a unique China model. [54] The power of adaptability is a direct result of effective system capabilities. These capabilities make any political system viable. So, without properly deploying these capabilities, no political system can run successfully.

In the global village, foreign direct investment through exports shows the effectiveness of distributive capability intact. Symbolic capability exposes the integration of a state through symbols, monuments, slogans, words, and achievements. Responsive capability is an output function that explores the people's response towards its system. The response is always according to the activity of the first four capabilities (see details ahead). If those capabilities have been utilized timely and effectively, the response will be accordingly or vice versa.

All capabilities have their mutual implications both at domestic and global levels. The developed world acquired these capabilities for centuries. The developing world, on the contrary, had remained for long under the thumb of the colonial powers, like France, Japan, Portugal, Spain, the U.K., and the U.S. Therefore, the South needed homework and a proper infrastructure for taking advantage of globalization. Dependency theory is an old saga; crying over the spilled milk is useless. It is the call of the day that the South has to adopt practical and pragmatic measures to meet international standards. This world will not listen to the people protesting and demonstrating against globalization; it will perish them. It will only assist in the survival of the fittest.

The countries under discussion, China and India, are two good examples of economic powers in Asia taking advantage of the prevailing world of globalization. Until 2014, the bubbling currents in China did not stir the outside world, specifically across the Pacific Ocean. In November 2014 and early 2015, Beijing announced $40 billion for the Silk Road and $46 billion for constructing the China Pakistan Economic Corridor (CPEC). China's massive spending on BRI immediately gained foreign attention.[55] The world accepts those who accept the rules of the prevailing global economy and wears a Golden Straitjacket (a term used for those countries who believe in neoliberalism).[56] All countries wear this Golden Straitjacket according to their system capability status. For example, India uses it a little.[57] China does not wear that jacket and has the power to shift the probability of economic advantage in its favor owing to its effective and active system capabilities.

Because of China's impressive strides in Artificial Intelligence (AI), Google chairman Eric Schmidt predicted that China will surpass the United States in AI by 2025. Although AI is not purely categorized as an arms race, it is portrayed as a significant medium. Like many other technologies, AI is neither governed nor controlled by any single power; therefore, it persists in being incorporated into diverse contexts. Chinese AI companies are traveling across Asian markets from Singapore to Tokyo. Many of the world's largest retail companies depend on dozens of Indian AI companies. On the one hand, these AI companies are dominating the Indian market. At the same time, on the other side, they have created global competition in numerous fields, such as medical diagnostics, computer vision, and consumer-based surveys. AI has evolved as a service across Asia, providing global governments and companies with extensive choices.[58]

Globalization is a multi-dimensional concept that speaks volumes about every aspect of the state: - economic, political, social, gender discrimination, environment, culture, and military. Therefore, it has a broader scope with umpteen directions. It is rapidly growing and keeps on changing every moment. The end of one research project may become old right after its completion. It is very possible that our research, the theme under discussion, may take different outlooks in the end. Hence, it is a very complex and demanding phenomenon. For example, democracy demands too much from individuals for their benefit. If individuals remain unsuccessful in fulfilling globalization's demands and needs, they have to suffer ultimately. Now, we proceed towards the scope of globalization for understanding this phenomenon on empirical lines.

Scope of Globalization

Globalization is an economic phenomenon, but the empirical study shows it is highly interdisciplinary. It is tough to appreciate globalization in the economic domain only. Political, social, gender discrimination, distinctive, and environmental degradation are other significant aspects also affected by this so-called new phenomenon. As mentioned in the last chapter, it was an old-age phenomenon, globalization, given a new catchy name. For convenience, we ascertain three significant domains of globalization: economic, political, and social.

Economic Globalization

Neoliberalism (end of state control of the economy) is the essence of today's global village. The economic aspect of globalization is reshaping global markets on a rapid scale. The capabilities of the political system can be considered as a scale of economic, political, or social development. The natural and material sources can also be considered a scale to measure any development in the political system. Economic globalization means an increased interconnectedness of IFIs, WTO, and MNCs. The democratization of finance through plastic money has compressed space and time. The use of credit cards has become a routine matter in the modern world; therefore, it has become easy for individuals to perform economic activities without any threat of robbery.

Yet, the striking feature here is the post-Cold War era, which is 'multi-cultural' and even 'multi-civilized' to a considerable extent. The center of power has also been divided into many states.[59] Kenichi Ohmae supports Huntington's idea of a borderless world where no country has a bar upon the flow of capital, goods, or services because of the communication revolution. Information technology has diminished the frontiers of many nations, allowing them to overcome the world's economic market.[60] National interests have become a declining industry in the world of politics.

The multipolar competition represents the purest version of the global system. Numerous countries' centers of gravity focus on filtering ideas, recycling capital, and adopting technology to boost their economies. Europe buttressed from colonizing Asia, and Asia amassed profit from American and European outsourcing. The infusions of Asian investment and talent make the most of the United States and European profits.[61]

Economic globalization has given a competitive boost to developed countries to pursue a race of economic monopolization on the world stage. Benjamin R. Barber opines that economic globalization, or globalization as a thoroughly modern phenomenon, seems impracticable owing to the heterogeneous character of the world. In every part of the world, ethnic races and tribes conflict with each other, so it is almost impossible to make uniform under the forces of McWorld or Jihad.[62] This jungle-like world is a whole of ethnic identities fighting with each other, for example, Kurds in Iraq, rival groups in Afghanistan, Quebec in Canada, Tamil in Sri Lanka, Serbians and Croats in former Yugoslavia, etc.

McWorld sometimes disguises itself under the name of democracy and gets hold of predacious markets. Jihad can also disguise itself under the cover of self-determination to escape from combative interests.[63] Jihad emerged as a counterforce against colonialism and imperialism and their economic offspring, capitalism, and modernity.

Owing to economic globalization, agriculture has become another source of economic development. For the developing states, in particular, the Third World states' agro-economy is an inevitable source of survival, but, unfortunately, it cannot extract its resources efficiently compared to the developed world. The developed world extracts much from its agriculture sector, using a fraction of its GDP.[64] Therefore, the developed world is not very concerned about agricultural products. In contrast, the developing world lacks resources due to a lack of scientific development and technological know-how. That is why the developing world is highly dependent upon the developed world. A country cannot flourish until it sufficiently delivers basic amenities of life to its people; the poorer states remain subservient to the rich even for food and natural resources. By that virtue, the developing world has no option but to look towards the industrialized states despite being agrarian polities. Another source that assists the phenomenon of globalization is the IFIs.

International financial institutions pretty much support globalization. The Bretton Woods institutions, the World Bank (WB) and the International Monetary Fund (IMF), have considered globalization a source of economic development. The reality exposes the unfair and partial attitudes of the twin Bretton Woods institutions.

By custom, the president of the World Bank is taken from the U.S., and the managing director of the funds has always been a European. The Americans always support this custom strongly and even want to have their managing director of the Fund. Such intentions mention the insincerity on the part of the United States.

The hard conditionalities of these financial institutions are threatening the developing world.

Political Globalization

The disintegration of the U.S.S.R. in 1991 gave rise to America as the sole superpower in the world. Instead of changing the political scenario, George Bush, the forty-second American President, introduced his New World Order in the early 1990s, in which free trade, human rights, and democracy were significant ideals. Since President Xi's coming to power, seven small leading groups have been organized in the party leadership to manage finance, law, and regional economies. [65]Political globalization is a modern philosophy based on neoliberal ideology, the colonialization of life, and mass consumption. It also supports democratic ideals and emphasizes their immediate implementation in the global environment of sovereign entities.

The dominance of democracy as a model of decision-making is the essence of political globalization. Therefore, it can be derived that political globalization is an amalgam of market and democracy. It is said that globalization has ended the traditional divide between the First World (which consists of the developed industrial world), the second, a communist World, and the poor Third World.

Political globalization affects different political systems in different ways. Some are traditional democracies (including developed world democratic nation-states), and others are transitional (including developing world democracies). Therefore, traditional democracies always try to dominate transitional democracies.

Meanwhile, Asia is in its early phase of globalization; therefore, it is too early to contemplate how major geopolitical, economic, social, and technological transformations will shape the present global Asianization. The coming decades will determine whether societies will adopt technocratic governance, capitalism, and social conservatism. Nor can it be forecasted how the West will respond to Asia's rise in the future.[66]

Capitalism tries to manufacture the needs of people and manipulate their sense and sensibility.[67] The essence of democracy does not lie in controlling the minds of people by alluring them through different means of advertisement or marketing. Democracy gives an individual a free hand to think over anything he wants and make a free judgment with his thoughts without any pressure. The industrialized world is interested in hurried pursuits of free markets without considering the consequences that may jeopardize democracy in the newly independent nations. McWorld is not a relief for all waning economies. Instead, it assists in undermining sustainable economies, as happened in the case of Germany after the ramification. It could not even evolve into a democratic society in Germany, so "McWorld is a problem, not a solution."[68]

As an economic force, McWorld wishes to introduce a liberal and free-market system under the umbrella of democracy. Realizing the authenticity of democratic ideals for the development of any political system is a hard nut to crack. China has an authoritarian system that bounces back the commercial and free-market forces without consideration and has emerged as an economic giant in Southeast Asia. Acculturation is not the solution to the problem. The countries which import democracy, multiparty parliamentary system, usually lack the capabilities, and resources to build a civil society that allows the democratic political institutions to work effectively.[69]" Without Civil Society, there can be no citizens, and thus no meaningful democracy."[70] McWorld is facing opposition from its counter-force Jihad. It (Jihad) is not giving much room to McWorld for its rapid development in the world.[71]

In the post-national era, it seems that McWorld and Jihad have been unsuccessful in creating a peaceful society. Jihad's (bloody revolution) and McWorld's (commercial or market revolution) modes of action obstruct human liberty. Jihad and McWorld need to be antagonistic to democracy but should support it in the prevailing circumstances.[72]

Hence, it becomes clear that homogenous societies can quickly be democratized compared to heterogeneous societies. Robert Putnam also believes that homogenous societies can develop democratic ideals and civic and political institutions.[73]

McWorld is doing its best to impose its liberal philosophy upon heterogeneous societies through its fastest music (MTV), fastest food (McDonald's), and fastest computers (Macintosh). It is almost impossible to harness the transitional societies with a modern cart of McWorld.

After the disintegration of the Soviet Union, America, along with its allies, desired to inject democratic norms into the societies of Eastern Europe and Russia as well. America has had success in a significant manner. Still, Asian societies like Vietnam, Central American societies like Cuba, and East Asian societies like China loathe democratic ideals and denounce any global policy against the very idea of their societies.

The Austro-Hungarians and the Russians are highly heterogeneous societies that hardly brook any bloodshed owing to the McWorld and jihad. Jihad is based upon two rabid versions, anti-pluralist and antimodern, "that has turned the rout of communist imperialism into a victory for irredentism and genocide and left democracy out in the cold."[74]

In Serbia, Croatia, Bulgaria, Mongolia, Lithuania, Belarus, Ukraine, Poland, and Hungary, free elections were held, and new governments assumed powers with old communists in the parliament, waiting for the meager and unroofed political institutions since there was no civil society in such countries to save and secure democratic ideals.[75]

Socialist Russia has met its account by political globalization; in his official address to the federal assembly in 1994, Yeltsin uttered the following words; "Without a developed civil society, state power inevitably takes on a despotic, totalitarian character. Only owing to civil society is this power subject to serving the individual and becomes a protection mechanism for freedom."[76]

The president's address exposes the hopelessness of the socialist system and the over-wheeling of capitalism. The prevailing situation in Russia gives a faded reality that it (Russia) will be a socialist or capitalist country. The question of democracy remains in the backdrop.[77] Capitalism has become opium for the Russians, keeping them very much possessive, even if it will keep them shaky until the political and social death of the Russians.[78] The reunification of West and East Germany is another success story of McWorld. In November 1989, unification came into existence to swallow up the East.[79] Germany is still suffering from the economic fallout.[80]

It can be synthesized that McWorld or Jihad is the opposite force trying to globalize the world in its unique style. On the contrary, each Islamic or modern society resists them and exposes the weakness of these forces and the rigidness of the local norms and values. America wishes to liberate the world economy as it has its ax to grind. China, on the other hand, is challenging McWorld with its socialist economy. Bangladesh, India, Maldives, Nepal, Pakistan, Sri Lanka, and other heterogeneous countries, which indulge in acculturation, political institutions cannot create a civil society that can nurture democracy in the long run.

Democracy is a gradual process that flourishes with time. Traditional democracies like Britain, Switzerland, and America had to sacrifice a lot to gain democratic ideals, and hundreds of years were needed to achieve democracy. Nevertheless, flames of discontent existed in such societies.[81]

"Neither Jihad nor McWorld promises a remotely democratic future."[82] In Afghanistan, the Taliban are posing that Jihad is a force that can deter any infidel system. The fact is that a power struggle is going on in Afghanistan, causing heavy causalities over innocent masses. Jihad does not mean to deprive the people of their fundamental rights. Islamic jihad is entirely different from the jihad introduced by Benjamin R. Barber in *Jihad Vs. McWorld*. The same situation is in Palestine, India, and Kashmir. In the name of religion, people have been killed. No one is imposing economic or political sanctions to deter Israelis and Indians from stopping violence against Muslims in Palestine, India, and Kashmir. If McWorld or Benjamin's Jihad is looking for integration in their unique style, why are they silent on Kashmir and Palestine issues?

A magical wand cannot install democracy overnight. The success stories of democracies show that it is a slow process; certain evolutionary stages give maturity to its culmination. Therefore, the people who wish to construct a global democracy need patience, tolerance, and a sense of equality, which is necessary to realize Ricardo's comparative advantage.[83] "Patience, political will, and boldness: not an easy combination of traits to cultivate, above all when democracy is under duress."[84] Now we see how cultural globalization is affecting the global village.

Cultural Globalization

Globalization culture means the globalization of norms, values, rights, and duties and, ultimately, constructing a civil society. Scientific knowledge and technological developments are the significant characteristics that shape the *fundamental character of human societies.*[85] The propaganda of human rights, civic culture, democracy, peace, and feminism are such forces that have transformed traditional societies altogether.

Due to shared ethnicity, diasporas serve as catalysts to strengthen external ties to their home countries. However, internal factors such as domestic resistance and policymakers' aversion are essential factors that can hinder the liberalization process. Additionally, as these diasporas build broader ties to domestic actors, they are more likely to transfer ideas and resources based on ethnic loyalties than nonethnic foreigners. [86]

Countries like Bangladesh, Bhutan, China, India, Maldives, Nepal, Pakistan, Sri Lanka, etc., borrow the social values of the modern or traditional world through McWorld. This may cause rifts, chaos, and political instability in developing countries. Therefore, it would be better to let developing countries evolve their own culture without any external pressure. The developed world has a vital interest in sabotaging the indigenous values of the Third World. Those vital interests are purely economic and political.[87]

The global recognition of Asian artistic output is another significant source of cultural convergence. Contemporary Asian arts are emerging globally through museums, galleries, and marvelous paintings. This global circulation of arts complements Western collections, too. Asia's leading cities are endeavoring their level best to become cultural hubs, such as the annual Art Basel Week in Hong Kong, Taipei's Songshan Cultural Park, and the 798 Art Zone of Beijing are a few examples. Additionally, adopting Western rituals like wild dance festivals and YouTube viral videos has fanned Asian culture outward. The cultural blending is also reflected in Asian food, ranging from the smoky grilled lamb of Central Asia to Southeast Asian coconut milk. Incorporating Asian taste into McDonald's menu, such as masala dosa burgers for Indians and shrimp burgers for Japanese, is a reminder for the West that in Asia, one must become Asian.[88]

The ongoing pressure of social globalization exposes the helplessness of human freedom. Although Kant and Hegel believe that the end of history may occur when true freedom of consciousness exists on earth,[89] The developed world goes against the democratic and free norms, adopts a monopoly of production and capital, and noticeably dominates world society with its financial capital. Capital accumulated by banks and employed by industrialists.[90] Hegel opines that the nature of human desire differs from society to society and culture to culture. For example, he says that a resident of America, France, or Japan lives in luxury in modern times but not in the earlier period. On the contrary, the residents of the Third World remain busy in the pursuit of security and food even in this modern time.[91]

The developed world intentionally shows itself as a model to the developing world to convince it of its imitation.[92] Global business strategies are no more similar to those centuries ago. It is nearly impossible for any nation to accrue the benefits of globalization by avoiding MNCs.[93] So, it prevails the Western political and cultural hegemony that gives a partial and ambiguous picture of political development since it only represents the Western model of political development.[94] Spengler and Toynbee have described the downfall of Western values and institutions in this century.[95] Therefore, it is a gross infringement on the part of the developed world that compulsorily imposes economic and political sanctions on the developing world. Cultural globalization has not only been deteriorating the social system of the transitional democracies. Japan is a traditional country where, at present, McDonald's and KFC are the most celebrated restaurants and earn a lot more than the local restaurants.[96] A few Japanese protest against the McWorld, but the youngsters like McWorld very much.[97] They are fond of the complex music of MTV and STAR channels. If they want to refresh themselves, they take Pepsi or Coke to serve their purpose.[98]

Both McWorld and Jihad threaten democratic ideals from the world stage.[99] Vladimir V. Zhirinovsky was cautious against cunning McWorld by recalling the harsh memories of two world wars when Germans assaulted in violent actions. Still, Americans were smart enough to infiltrate through cosmetic outcries of democracy and human rights.[100] They know invading with chewing gum, stockings, and McDonald's is better.[101] McWorld and Jihad both are trying their best to capture the world without considering the aspirations of people. McWorld emphasizes commercial trends and jihad preaches for bloody revolution against all infidels. McWorld is a dangerous force in the long run as it is a kind of velvet revolution and diffuses into society without making it conscious. Therefore, societies become helpless against McWorld owing to the strong tentacles of the free market, fast music, computers, and fast-food restaurants.

Jihad is a violent force. Liberal societies protest against it. Sometimes, clerical societies welcome McWorld more than Jihad. Pakistan, Iran, Egypt, and the Middle East are countries where McWorld has deep roots. Jihad can be seen in Afghanistan, Chechnya, Bosnia, and Kosovo.

Western influence has deteriorated some countries' cultural and social values. The Cable TV programs have drastically impressed the masses in Third World countries and eradicated indigenous social values, replacing them with Western culture and norms. For example, Iran is a conservative country importing satellite programs, which are wiping out the religious and cultural values of Iran.[102] The skeptics in Iran are condemning the ongoing influence of satellite programs that Western imperialists have prepared. Lip service is being paid "to learn the import, manufacture, and use of satellite dishes."[103]It is now evident that history gives us Jihad as a counterforce for McWorld, and individuals can't live in both domains at the same time. They have to choose one domain, undoubtedly, and sadly, individuals are looking for a sad society along with democrats.[104] It is a known fact that both Jihad and McWorld do not give much room to democracy.[105]

Under its cosmetic language of choice, McWorld hardly allows people to buy or sell at their own will. Advertising and marketing have bound people to buy a few popular company brands. The IMF and World Bank are said to promote markets, but they always work for democracy. Both IFIs have sacrificed civic balance and social equality to attain economic goals.[106]

Environmental Degradation Resulting from Globalization

The degradation of the environment is another aspect of cultural globalization that has damaged the Third World. Maurice F. Strong emphasizes that we should consider environmental changes that have resulted from ecological, commercial, and technological advancements that have polluted the environment to exterminate the resource for future generations. It is against the concept of sustainable human development.[107] Geoffrey Palmer, another environmental protection proponent, urges to have institutional and legal mechanisms "to deal effectively with transboundary and biosphere environmental degradation…We lack institutions capable of ensuring that our rules are effective."[108]

Climate change will not only accelerate globalization processes in the form of mutual efforts due to the global nature of a problem but also promote Asianization. For example, the doubling of Russia's harvests in the last decade has tripled its exports. Its exports to South and East Asia have grown to 60 percent annually. Besides attracting East Asian importers like China and Korea, Iraq, Syria, Saudi Arabia, and Iran are more likely to become its wheat importers due to crippling droughts predicted on account of regional climate fluctuations.[109]

Cultural globalization seeks a transnational form of sovereignty that may come from a transnational identity group. However, it is hard to find any form of international civil society; even in a sovereign entity, citizenship precedes civic institutions.

In such a state of affairs, how can a global citizen look for global democracy?[110] The phenomenon of cultural globalization is working very smoothly under the Western market strategy, which reached not only the homes of Russia but also every home of the developing world, affecting innocent minds through video games, comics, characters, attitudes, violence, consumption, victory, and sex, etc.[111]

In the light of previous comparative studies, the role of political forces and institutions is placed central but on the contrary, globalization literature underscores the role of MNCs and international organizations to transform China and India economically. The social network theory (SNT) views China's entrepreneurial diaspora to be significant in accelerating FDI liberalization, whereas, in India, policymakers eschewed quick opening to FDI due to the influence of local businesses.[112]

Barber opines that creating a civic society is based upon the active participation of the people in a state. Their participation, vigilance, dedication, and devotion to the political systems are the themes of a successful civic political system. The international community needs cooperation at the individual and collective levels that gives way to civil society. In turn, civil society needs an association based on friendship and mutual interest and "confederalism," categorically under the influence of member states.[113]

It is evident that without democracy, the terrors of Jihad and deficient McWorld can hardly compel human beings to cooperate to establish a global civic society. After closely examining the three main aspects of globalization (economic, political, and socio-cultural), it has become inevitable to see the changes in the developed and developing world to analyze the effects of this phenomenon in two worlds.

It can be deduced that globalization is the monopolization of economic, social, and political resources by the 'haves' at the cost of 'have-nots.' The NWO, the global village, is a global pillage through IFIs. Globalization is being utilized to the advantage of the developed world. The digital divide between the North and the South has created an imbalance on the world stage, which is why terrorism seems at the driving seat. "Megalothymia"[114] in the most industrialized world invokes a sense of deprivation in less developed nation-states. Natural inequality between the North and the South, and the status-conscious poor world is living under dependentia.

So, Francis Fukuyama's *The End of History* seems at stake emphatically as neo-colonialism has emerged in its cosmetic form. After theoretical conceptualization, we now assess globalization's impact in its operational form in China and India.

Endnotes

1 Parag Khanna, *THE FUTURE IS ASIAN: Commerce, Conflict, and Culture in the 21st Century*: Simon & Schuster, 2019, 8.

2 Thomas L. Friedman, *Understanding Globalization: The Lexus and The Olive Tree*, New York: Anchor Books, INC., 1999, 14.

3 Parag Khanna, *THE FUTURE IS ASIAN: Commerce, Conflict, and Culture in the 21st Century*: Simon & Schuster, 2019, 25.

4James H. Mittelman, *Globalization Syndrome: Transformation and Resistance*, New Jersey: Princeton University press, 2000., 16.

5 Richard D'Aveni, *Hypercompetition: Managing the Dynamics of Strategic Maneuvering*, New York: Free Press, 1994, cited in Mittelman, *The Globalization Syndrom*, 16.

6 Min Ye, *The Belt Road and Beyond: State-Mobilized Globalization in China: 1998-2018*: Cambridge University Press, 2020,27.

7 Friedman, *Understanding Globalization*, 72.

8 Ibid.

9 Parag Khanna, *THE FUTURE IS ASIAN: Commerce, Conflict, and Culture in the 21st Century*: Simon & Schuster, 2019, 114.

10 Kenichi Ohmae, *The End of the Nation States: The Rise of Regional Economies*, New York: Simon and Schuster Inc., 1996, 1-5.

11 Ibid.

12 Min Ye, *Diasporas and Foreign Direct Investment in China and India*: Cambridge University Press, 2014, 05.

13 Parag Khanna, *THE FUTURE IS ASIAN: Commerce, Conflict, and Culture in the 21st Century*: Simon & Schuster, 2019, 95.

14 Ibid.

15 Min Ye, *Diasporas and Foreign Direct Investment in China and India*: Cambridge University Press, 2014, 113.

16 Kenichi Ohmae, "Big 3: No Longer Solely American," *Detroit News*, April 21, 1985.

17 Kenichi Ohmae, Deficit Myths, *Wall Street Journal*, July 30, 1985.

18 Harry Magdoff, *The Age of Imperialism*, New York: Modern Reader Paperback Edition, 1969, 27.

19 Barber, *Jihad Vs McWorld*, 10.

20 Ibid., 17.

21 Ibid., 13.

22 Ibid.

23 Former Secretary of State George Shultz, cited by Winston, Twilight, 10.

24 Cited in Louis Uchitelle, "Gillette's World View: One Blade Fits All," *The New York Times*, January 3, 1994.

25 Barber, *Jihad Vs McWorld*, 23.

26 Ibid.

27 Ibid., 24.

28 Ibid., 18.

29 Kenichi Ohmae, *Troid Power*, New York: Free Press, 1985, 27.

30 Ibid., 28.

31 Parag Khanna, *THE FUTURE IS ASIAN: Commerce, Conflict, and Culture in the 21st Century*: Simon & Schuster, 2019, 161.

32 The American MNGs are working very efficiently in the developing world. They are earning at the stake of local markets and sending back all profits in their native lands that are billions of dollars every year. In this way these MNGs are not only grasping over the world's economic markets but also capturing the local labor cunningly.

33 Barber, *Jihad Vs McWorld*, 31.

34 "That is what a market is: an unobstructed set of change relationships among individuals, consumers and individual producers that are allowed to take its course; and McWorld is nothing if not a market." Ibid., 28-29

35 Ibid., 32.

36 Who will stand up to the IMF for reform? German Newspaper News Service, *The New Vision*, 27 September 1999, 2.

37 International Monetary Fund, Good Governance: The IMF's Role, 2nd March 2000, preamble, 1.

38 Ibid., Para-6.

39 Grey Mills, "The Future of Globalization," *South African Journal of International Affairs*, Vol. 6, No. 1 (1981), 83.

40 IMF, Annual Report 1997, 59-60.

41 David Katona, "Challenging the World Global Structure through Self Determination: An African Perspective," *AmericanUniversity International Law Review*, Vol. 14, No. 6 (1998), 1458-1462.

42 Smith and Moises Naim, Altered States: Globalization, Sovereignty, and Governance, Ottawa, International Development Research Council, 2000, 17. "The functional argument for transparency and accountability is equally important. No institution of authority now can long endure without the informed consent of those who are governed by it. Globalization is arming people with the information they need to consent to those who are cases, the means to refuse it. But lack of a democratic process is keeping international institutions weak. People living in democracies are understandably reluctant to transfer allegiance and powers to organizations less accountable (and even more remote) than their own national governments." Ibid.

43 Barber, *Jihad Vs McWorld*, 60.

44 Ibid., 24.

45 The new universalism is little more than an omnipresent American parochialism

dubbed into various languages and funded by multinational corporations.

46 Min Ye, *The Belt Road and Beyond: State-Mobilized Globalization in China: 1998-2018*: Cambridge University Press, 2020,86.

47 Parag Khanna, *The Future is Asian: Commerce, Conflict, and Culture in the 21st Century*: Simon & Schuster, 2019, 179-180.

48 Friedman, *Understanding Globalization*, 158.

49 Ibid.

50 Ibid., 137.

51 Ibid., 135.

52 Ibid.

53 Ibid., 104.

54 Min Ye, *The Belt Road and Beyond: State-Mobilized Globalization in China: 1998-2018*: Cambridge University Press, 2020,04.

55 Min Ye, *The Belt Road and Beyond: State-Mobilized Globalization in China: 1998-2018*: Cambridge University Press, 2020,04.

56 Friedman, *Understanding Globalization*, 104.

57 Ibid., 108.

58 Parag Khanna, *THE FUTURE IS ASIAN: Commerce, Conflict, and Culture in the 21st Century*: Simon & Schuster, 2019, 186.

59 Samuel P. Huntington, The Clash of Civilizations and The Remaking of World Order, New Delhi, Penguin Book India Pvt. Ltd., 1996, 20.

60 Kenichi Ohmae, *The End of the Nation States,* 1.

61 Parag Khanna, *THE FUTURE IS ASIAN: Commerce, Conflict, and Culture in the 21st Century*: Simon & Schuster, 2019, 320.

62 The McWorld can be considered as a unifying force, introduced by the West, but has its antithesis in the form of Jihad, which is a purely Muslim unifying force. Benjamin R. Barber emphasizes that both Jihad and McWorld wage war on the sovereign state and are undermining the democratic institutions in the nation-states.

63 Barber, *Jihad Vs McWorld,* 10.

64 Ibid., 33-34.

65 Min Ye, *The Belt Road and Beyond: State-Mobilized Globalization in China: 1998-2018*: Cambridge University Press, 2020,209.

66 Parag Khanna, *THE FUTURE IS ASIAN: Commerce, Conflict, and Culture in the 21st Century*: Simon & Schuster, 2019, 320-321.

67 Barber, *Jihad Vs McWorld,* 15.

68 Ibid.

69 Ibid., 234.

70 Ibid.

71 "There does not finally seem to be much hope for traditional institutions as saviors of democracy on a transnational scale in an era poised between jihad and McWorld. Europe, which has increases significant economic integration organized around regional councils, parliaments, and courts, still lacks democratic credibility with the citizen of its member countries." Ibid., 231.

72 Ibid., 232.

73 Robert Putnam, *Making Democracy Work: Civic Tradition in Modern Italy,* Princeton: Princeton University Press, 1993, 243.

74 Barber, *Jihad Vs McWorld,* 196.

75 Ibid., 197.

76 "Rule of Law for civil society, "Paper prepared for the XVI World Congress of the International Political Science Association in Berlin, August 1994, 10.

77 Barber, *Jihad Vs McWorld,* 257.

78 Ibid., 255.

79 Ibid., 261-262.

80 Ibid.

81 Ibid., 278-79.

82 Ibid., 220.

83 Ibid., 224.

84 Ibid.

85 Francis Fukuyama, The End of History and the Last Man, Avon Books, 1993, 72.

86 Min Ye, *Diasporas and Foreign Direct Investment in China and India*: Cambridge University Press, 2014, 40.

87 The so-called modernization is making the developing world extremely vulnerable and dynamic. The military threat forces, even the developed world, have to adopt defensive modernization, a concept coined to reform the sovereign entity under the pretext of military threat. Walt Rustow has also explained the phenomenon that states sometimes have to reform themselves under military threats.….The classic example of defensive modernization can be seen in Russia when Mikhail Gorbachev introduced perestroika. The soviet officials openly declared that it had become inevitable for the Soviet Union to reconstruct the economy to cope with the prevailing world's economic and military prospects. Samuel P. Huntington, Political Order in Changing Societies, New Haven, Conn: YaleUniversity Press, 1968, 154-156.

88 Parag Khanna, *THE FUTURE IS ASIAN: Commerce, Conflict, and Culture in the 21st Century*: Simon & Schuster, 2019, 305-307.

89 Fukuyama, *The End of History and the Last Man,* 60.

90 Kant emphasizes, "The History of the world is none other than the progress of the consciousness of freedom." He says human freedom lies in the modern constitutional state or liberal democracy. Ibid.

91 "Our present desires are conditioned by our social milieu, which in turn is the product

of the entirety of our historical past." Ibid., 65.

92 Karl Max writes in the preface of *Das Kapital*, "The Country that is more developed industrially only shows, to less developed, the image of its own future." Ibid., 68

93 Min Ye, *Diasporas and Foreign Direct Investment in China and India*: Cambridge University Press, 2014, 114.

94 Mark Kesselman, "Order or Movement? The literature of Political development as Ideology." World Politics 26, No.1 (October 1973), 139-154

95 Fukuyama, *The End of History and the Last Man*, 70

96 Barber, *Jihad Vs. McWorld,*192

97 ibid., 192-193

98 "They shake their local folk zithers at a centralist and encroaching French or German or Japanese culture they despise and then hammer out the tunes of an even more centralist and encroaching global culture on their quaint instruments." Ibid., 194.

99 "The outcome inside their struggling souls will likely condition the outcome for global civilization, whose prospects, consequently, do not seem terribly missing." Ibid.

100 Ibid., 198.

101 Celestine Bohlen, "Zhirinovsky Cult Grows," *The New York Times,* April 5, 1994. AI, 12. In Eastern and Central Europe and the republic of the erstwhile Soviet Union, forces of Jihad affect the political and economic institutions, but no success story has been observed. Also see Barber, *Jihad Vs. McWorld,* 198.

102 Chris Hedger, "Tehran Journal", *The New York Times*, August 16, 1994. A2.

103 Leslie Planner and Cherry Mosteher, "Bringing a Beam of sleight to the Closed World of Iran", *The Guardian*, August 5, 1994, 14.

104 Barber, *Jihad Vs McWorld*, 216.

105 Ibid.

106 Ibid., 221.

107 Maurice F. Strong, "ECO' 92: Critical Challenges and Global Solutions" *Journal of International Affairs,* No 44, 1991, 287-298.

108 Geoffrey Palmer, "New Ways to Make International Law," *American Journal of International Law,* No.86, 1992, 259.

109 Parag Khanna, *THE FUTURE IS ASIAN: Commerce, Conflict, and Culture in the 21st Century*: Simon & Schuster, 2019, 85.

110 Martha Nussbaum, "Patriotism or Cosmopolitanism? Martha Nussbaum in Debae," *Boston Review,* Special issue, Volume XIX, Number 5, October, November 1914.

111 Barber, *Jihad Vs. McWorld,*

112 Min Ye, *Diasporas and Foreign Direct Investment in China and India*: Cambridge University Press, 2014, 205.

113 "That is well rooted in civil society, and no citizens for whom the other is not synonymous with the enemy; civil society is products of a democratic way of life." Ibid., 291.

114 According to Plato, Megalothymia and Isothymia are two important parts of our soul. In our opinion, Microthymia is also the third and very important part of our soul, which means considering ourselves inferior to others is really the nucleus of all problems. The Third World, which is the victim of Microthymia, can hardly cope with the ongoing flow of globalization thanks to its weak and inefficient capabilities. As noted above, those capabilities of a political system could be considered a scale for political development in any nation-state. The MNGs have undermined the local business of the countries. The borderless world of Ohmae and McWorld of Barber categorically explain the psychological abduction of this generation.

Chapter 2. China and Globalization: Attributes

China is the most populous country in the world. It is emerging as an economic giant in the twenty-first century. Despite its controlled and commanded economy, China is making significant development in its socio-political and economic domains. Her modern approach towards world politics is based on opening up its economy for world trade. The question is: Can China have a consistent economic growth rate without substantial political reforms? Why are political reforms necessary for China? Do political reforms directly correlate with economic and social development? How will China perform before and after the age of globalization? How does globalization make an impact on Chinese economic, political, and social spheres? Along with these major queries, in-depth interviews with Chinese socio-political and economic think tanks are also included in this chapter.

On December 11, 2001, China became a member of the WTO and started exporting its consumer goods from labor-intensive low-tech to capital-intensive high-tech worldwide by significantly reducing import tariffs and canceling various non-tariff measures.

China has a hard-working population that believes more in approaching collectivism through individualism. China realizes that real independence can only be achieved through economic prosperity. China gives a lot of importance to its individuals by obliging them to participate in the system to flourish independently, not dependently. It enhances the participatory culture in China that was hardly found before Deng Xiaoping. This is encouraged by the government through a policy of modernization, yet without losing its traditional values.

The World Investment Report of 2006 compares the FDI liberalization of China and India in 1990 and 2004, which shows that China was persistently a frontrunner in 1990, and its ranking improved till 2004. Still, on the other side, India's ranking fell in the aforementioned period.[1]

In the mid-1970s, China started modernization. Modernization in China can be seen in three political, economic, and social domains. We can say that modernization is a movement from rural to urban, religion to secular, agriculture to industrial, authoritarian to democratic, illiteracy to literacy, and ignorance of media participation.

According to Lerner, "The principal aspects of modernization, urbanization, industrialization, democratization, education, and media participation do not occur in haphazard and unrelated fashion."[2] They mostly occur unconsciously but usually go together owing to some historical sense.[3] There are five levels of political modernization: psychological, intellectual, demographic, social, and economic.[4]

The psychological level of modernization shows a fundamental transformation in Chinese values, attitudes, and expectations. A traditional individual believes in the natural continuity of society and does not intend to change or control it. On the other hand, a modern individual intends to change society and wants to adapt it according to the prevailing circumstances. Lerner says that a modern man has a "mobile personality" that adjusts everything according to his own heart.

The intellectual level elaborates on the fact about the extensive knowledge of Chinese social capital about the precincts. It all happened through the revolution in mass media, an increase in literacy level, and education.

Demographic level gives the details of modernization in the context of a healthy increase in health and life expectancy, increased occupational and demographic mobility from the periphery to core[5] in China.

Asia's pre-modern globalization has been helpful for even Europe in gaining weaponry and navigation knowledge that it later on used on Chinese and Indian trade routes.[6] Social mobilization in China organizes people more effectively to make the secondary organization participate in society for different functions. The traditional authoritative system based on "cumulative inequalities" gives way to democratic values based on "dispersed inequalities."[7]

The rise of China in the world economic system has not merely accelerated globalization but also shifted power and world development trajectories.[8] The economic level of modernization involves diversified activities, consisting of simple occupations that replace complex ones; sustenance agriculture replaces market agriculture. Again, agriculture surrenders before commercial, industrial, and other activities.[9]

The above-mentioned five levels of modernization give us two main categories of modernization:

- Social mobilization is achieved through increased literacy and education, communication revolution, mass media, multimedia exposure, and urbanization. Karl Deutsch's social mobilization is the process by which "major clusters of old social, economic, and psychological commitments are eroded or broken, and people become available for new patterns of socialization and behaviors."[10] This is what is going on in China in the twenty-first century.

- Economic modernization based upon the uplift of economic activity and output of society. The per capita income, gross national product, and levels of industrialization can be instrumental in measuring the economic development of any country. Besides it; a rise in life expectancy, caloric intake, and several doctors and hospitals are indicators that depict the individual's welfare in the modernization process.[11]

Social mobilization focuses on the transformation of individuals', groups', and societies' ambitions, while economic modernization concentrates on changing their capabilities. The empirical study infers three major aspects of political modernization.

First, it involves national unity and centralization only through the recognized law-making institutions. Second, it involves the differentiation of functions with specialized structures like legal, military, administrative, and scientific structures that are autonomous and specialized but, even then, are subservient to the real sovereign. Third, it involves increased participation of people in politics that may enhance the control of government by the people in the modern age. Therefore, rationalizations of authority, specialized structures, and increased participation are the main characteristics of modern society.[12] It would be an oversimplification to say that only rationalization of authority, structural differentiation, and mass participation in political modernization.

There is a difference between defining political modernization as a movement from a traditional to a modern polity and political modernization as the "political aspects and political effects of social, economic and cultural modernization."[13] Political modernization as a movement from traditional to modern polity explains the desirable direction of political change, while political modernization as the political aspects and effects denotes the changes occurring in modern society.

> "Modernization means that all groups, old as well as new, traditional as well as modern, become increasingly aware of themselves as groups and of their interests and claims about other groups. One of the most striking phenomena of modernization, indeed, is the increased consciousness, coherence, organization, and action which it produces in many social forces which existed on a much lower level of conscious identity and organization in traditional society."[14]

The former chairperson of Hongkong and Shanghai Banking Corporation Limited (HSBC), Stuart Gulliver, remarked, "The American dream of the 21st century is becoming the Asian dream of the 21st: A house, a car, a smartphone, travel, banking services, health care the prospect of unfettered upward social mobility for many more families."[15]

Owing to a highly interdisciplinary approach, globalization affects all domains of a political system. The international political environment allows such systems to survive and efficiently utilize their 'system capabilities'. The capability to adapt itself according to the international political environment is a key to success for transitional[16] countries. China, undoubtedly, has done well, especially after its membership in the WTO at the end of 2001. Here are the details that render China's efficacy of its 'system capabilities' in the twenty-first century.

Globalization and Its Impact on

China's political placement

China is a country emerging as an economic giant without democracy. It is interesting to see how Chinese political endeavor differs entirely from the Western world. Despite its centralized political system, China is making considerable development in fulfilling the needs and demands of the present generation in time without compromising the needs and demands of the future generation. China is governing its people without holding any formal democratic form of government. This shows that China tends to respect its people's fundamental rights. The West had exaggerated for the Tiananmen Massacre in 1989 that raised questions against Chinese respect for human rights in the international community.

Leadership, decentralization, and local government are attributed as major ingredients of China's domestic politics and significantly contribute to a transformative performance by diaspora entrepreneurs. For example, although Den Xiaoping did not propose FDI policies yet he encouraged diaspora influence. Rapidly FDI was encouraged in the coming years. Decentralization allowed the Chinese government to experiment with different economic practices.[17]

China has never been intellectually dependent on the West as compared to the rest of the transitional democracies of the developing world. China is confident in its own identity and skillful individuals. It is not afraid of its gigantic population size but keeps itself busy in utilizing that dexterous 'social capital' efficiently.

It is believed that democracy is the best form of government in the contemporary era as it guides the individual towards its end product, allows him to have its destination that may be Capitalism, Christianity, Communism, Hinduism, Islam, Judaism, Sinicism, Socialism, or any other ism. After contemplating objectively, the individual attains his real destination. We can derive that democracy is not an end product but an approach or guide to have its end product.

Globalization has changed the definition and basic ingredients of democracy. Today, democracy is a form of government that is represented by the people; it is not for the people, of the people. It means that in a democracy a small number of educated and wise people comprehend the problems of the common persons and have the urge to solve their problems by utilizing given resources. As we know, there are only a few individuals in any community who know their rights and duties. Therefore, such educated leaders or representatives of society talk about the welfare of the majority of the people.

In China, the Communist Party is solving partially the problems of the people and using more of their wisdom for the betterment of the Party. Chinese leaders are trying to understand the needs and demands of the people but react according to the directions of the Party. This is where China receives criticism from the West for the undemocratic nature of its political system.

Therefore, China is not convinced that democracy is a source of true individual liberty. Although she is attracting Western trade and investment, she is still away from democratic norms, as Minixin Pei admonishes in his article *The Dark Side of China*- "China's future will be decay, not democracy."[18] He thinks China can never become a politically viable and respected country without comprehensive political reforms.

China's political system has been closed. The hype about its liberalization is faster than its real trajectory.[19] China's political system is void of democratic flavor owing to its traditional outfit and conservative leadership that believes in authoritarianism.

The disintegration of the Soviet Union in 1991 and the collapse of Communism in Eastern Europe had a great impact on China. She decided to make some changes in her political placement that could restrain any political upheaval in the country.[20] Political democratization and economic liberalization were considered the sine qua non for the sustainability of the system. Political stability leads toward economic prosperity and wins foreign investment and confidence.[21]

In the Deng Xiaoping era, China did not go for any democratic revolution at once for fear that it might cause 'da luan' (great chaos). He talked about the professional bureaucracy that could steer the country towards peaceful development.[22] Initially, Western writers thought that Deng Xiaoping and Gorbachev were "restoring capitalism" in China and Russia.[23] On March 30, 1979, Deng Xiaoping delivered a historic address in which he persisted with modernization without democracy. He said that political reforms were indispensable for overcoming all economic crises. It was the call of the day to reorganize, readjust, and integrate ourselves by sacrificing personal interests for the welfare of the whole. Democracy might be disastrous for our system. We had to be watchful and vigilant in this respect.[24] It was a 'Mandate of Heaven' in China explained by Confucius' disciple Mencius that if an emperor could not fulfill the needs and demands of the people in time, the people had the right and a duty to unseat him.[25]

China adopted decentralization to control a huge population size effectively. It decentralized authority at a lower level, which enhanced economic development.[26] Local governments in China generated their revenue and carved out an investment plan that gave a boost to the Chinese economy.[27]

The Western writers talk about human rights violations in China and give an example of the Tiananmen Square massacre. Surprisingly, the same kind of incidents can also be seen in Thailand in 1976 at Thammasat University, in South Korea in 1980 at Kwangju, and in India in 1990 at Srinagar, but no hype could be found in the media against human rights violations.[28] Therefore, it seems that such incidents in developing countries are routine matters.

Today, no operational form of democracy can be seen in the contemporary world; so-called democratic states hold selective morality in their behavior. This jungle-like world where 'might is right is still working. Undoubtedly, the West and its allies all have opted for Islamic values in their true sense. Good governance, sustainable human development, and constitutional liberalism are pristine canons of Islam. These all are being observed factually in America, Australia, Canada, the UK, and other Western countries but with an amalgam of selective morality that is why these perfect standards of Islam (good governance, sustainable human development, and constitutional liberalism) have been disliked by the developing world.

Globalization made an impact on the Chinese political system in a positive way. It is competing with the international environment, adopting modernization of its unique style. It claims to be a communist country but acts well as a market socialist to adjust itself to the international environment.

China looks successful for the time being and attracts foreign direct investment (FDI) in an amazing way. It disguises itself well under the clout of market socialism to avoid anarchy at home as most Western countries, including America, claim to be a follower of capitalism, but they pursue a mixed economy. China is paying back in the same coins, answering the hype against the Tiananmen Square massacre with market socialism and enjoying membership of the WTO. All credit goes to the Chinese leadership and political infrastructure that remained active and on its guard to face the challenges of media hype.

The modern political system in China allows taking a leaf out of Western democracy's book for its advantages, not for its disadvantages. That is why the Chinese system has become invincible. The Chinese leadership is employing democratic advantages, leaving out its harmful aspects. Chinese experience of giving human rights is different from that of Russia and Eastern Europe. It persisted with individual rights and their duties to attain the welfare of the whole.[29] Russia and Eastern Europe were found guilty in that domain.

"The experiment' is the Chinese leaders' attempt to modernize China by opening its economy but holding political change in check."[30] Chinese know that introducing capitalism in China may cause chaos, therefore, they are very concerned about boosting the Chinese economy. Open elections have been in some villages and allowed many businessmen to join the Communist Party in the twenty-first century, but there is no opening up of the political system yet observed.[31] Few appointments of non-communist ministers like Wan Gang in April 2007 and Chen Zhu in June 2007 in science and technology and health ministries, respectively, show that globalization is working successfully in China.[32]

Friedman's 'Globalution'[33] (revolution from beyond) also remained at arm's length in the political system of China. He believes that MNCs like Merrill Lynch, Pizza Hut, PricewaterhouseCoopers, or other international organizations like WTO and ASEAN or some human rights organizations may create a revolution from beyond in some political systems where democracy does not exist.[34]

In the case of China, 'Globalution' could not work because of its leadership policies and reforms. For example, in 1979, there were no McDonald's in China,[35] but after the reforms of Deng Xiaoping, China had more than 200 McDonald's in 1996.[36] "The world's largest restaurant chain (McDonald's) owns and operates 595 outlets in China and plans to add as many as 120 a year..."[37] This food Chain has planned to increase its number by 1000 McDonald's in China ahead of the World Olympics in 2008.[38] Even increasing in number day by day very swiftly, Chinese policymakers are not allowing any MNC to work in China without a joint venture. This is where the Chinese are very smart for protecting their country from the effects of the 'globalution' and the "Golden Straight Jacket," the detail will come in the latter part of this chapter.

The narrative of global governance is also rebalanced by Asia's rise. Historically, Asia has been on the receiving end of global governance but now it plays an active role in shaping norms and providing public goods. The way United States' global military presence enabled other countries to keep their budgets down, China is also providing a development platform through low-cost infrastructure for dozens of countries.[39]

In the 1970s, globalization was not known in China. It started making reforms in its political system after 1980. China did that pragmatically but with increments and gradually started adjusting to the world environment and joined the WTO in 2001. During a visit to China, we find that this society is very cool in all respects. They are not in a hurry, not over-ambitious, but always looking for sustainable growth at individual and collective levels.

In the 1990s, globalization came into vogue in world politics; the fall of communism also took place in the same decade, so the international environment worked as a catalyst in the Chinese political system in making reforms; besides that, China was ready to face the challenge of globalization effectively as we all know that opportunity is always availed by the prepared mind. This is where China has always been different from the rest of the world. The Chinese leadership was aware of changing world affairs in the 1970s; therefore, they decided to have reforms well before any considerable transformation in world affairs.

Political intelligentsia in China does not believe in changing the Chinese political system at any cost. The Chinese Communist Party believes in changing its attitude rather than the form of government, as the West is not ready to change its biased and aggressive attitude toward weaker nations but wishes to have a so-called democratic system. Contrary to this, China has an authoritative and controlled political system with a flexible and adaptive outlook towards the world community in the twenty-first century. That was why the Chinese did not believe China should have political reforms.

The political economy of China exposes that political reforms are not necessary for economic development, but reformation in attitudes of the common person as well as the political elite is the sine qua non for sustainable economic growth. The contemporary Chinese economy candidly explains that the country's strong economy is the main concern for having a sustainable political system, but a sustainable political system may not guarantee a sustainable economy.

A strong economy comes from individuals' participation in the development of the country, and that participation can only be achieved through honest leadership. In China, political leaders like Mao, Deng, and others were successful in mobilizing people for national interests, and they consistently worked on lessening the gap between national and personal interests. That was where China became different from other countries in its political, economic, and social domains in the twenty-first century.

The creeping protectionism of American fist policies is equally alarming for Europe and Asia. To substitute the U.S., Eurasian ties have strengthened. China's diplomatic relations and annual joint sessions with Germany have also improved trade relations between the two countries. German chancellor, Angela Merkel's eight visits to China between 2004 and 2018 are evidence that European leaders travel more to Asia instead of the U.S. In 2018, Xi Jinping claimed to "open the door even wider" to German business. Moreover, Europe's countries' decision to join the Asian Infrastructure Investment Bank (AIIB), despite the United States' objections, divulges that Europe has reoriented its diplomatic and commercial weight to Asia.[40]

The Chinese Vice-Premier Wen Jiabao says, "The Chinese government has always dedicated to the establishment of a just and rational international economic order and will strive for this goal with unremitting efforts.... All countries, big or small, strong or weak, rich or poor, should have equal rights to participate in the formulation of the 'rule of games' in international affairs."[41] Therefore, it seems that the Chinese strategy towards globalization also aims to increase China's influence on world affairs in economic and political domains.

China usually does not support democracy because of its many versions, such as American democracy, Asian democracy, European democracy, or Western democracy. Therefore, it seems very uncomfortable to adopt a system with multiple faces. We also know that change in any system can occur through a small number of people. It never happens with a large number of people.

For making a change in any system, it is not the majority of people required, but a firm commitment on the part of a few people is necessary for the welfare of the whole. There are many examples in the world in this context. Abdul Sattar Edhi and Imran Khan in Pakistan and Mother Teresa in India are classic examples of who are not in the majority, but their commitment to serving people is firm. Mao and Deng in China are also good examples who create change in China single-handedly. In the same way, China believes that its political system does not buy the idea of democracy for the rule of the majority.

China's Economic Interests

China has a centralized command economy but after being a member of the WTO, it has relaxed many restrictions to be an economic giant in the international environment. After the U.S., today China is considered the second-largest economy in the world.[42] Particularly, the West portrays BRI as a Chinese hegemonic design contrary to its paradox of accelerating modernization and boosting the growth of countries [43] , however, the Chinese consider themselves at number four after the U.S., Japan, and Germany.

Synergism (The theological doctrine that salvation results from the interaction of human will and divine grace) is transforming the Chinese economy into a big giant in this century. Beijing believes in the economic strife of human beings through cumulative effect rather than the individual. It does not mean that individual is not important but his participant behavior is the call of the day in China.

China is extracting its economic resources at home and abroad- regulating, and distributing those resources quite adequately. Countries living in the age of globalization have to boost up their economies through interdependence and enhancing trade with other countries. The following table shows a success story for economic growth in China in the twenty-first century. The World Bank sources give details of the Chinese creeping economic growth rate in 2001 that was 7.1.

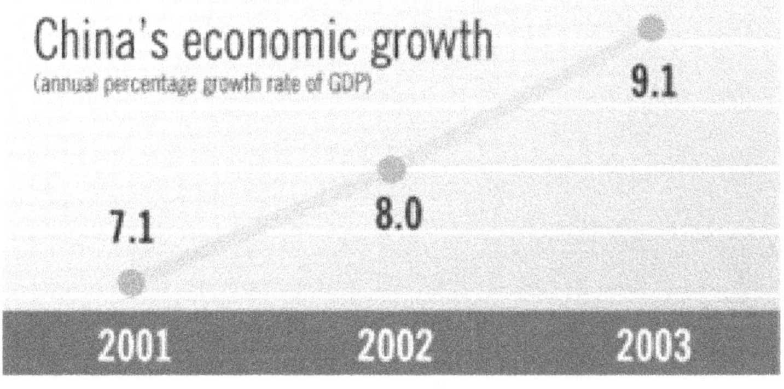

Source: World Bank.

In 2003, when other national economies began to fall back, China kept gathering speed with a GDP of 9.1 percent. The country's nearly unappeasable demand for raw materials has reinforced trade links with neighbors and commodity producers in the world. When China pronounced its intention to import a record volume of soybeans, for instance, prices increased as much as 28 percent in peripheral areas as in central Illinois. China's share of world exports, at 1.9 percent in 1990, reached 6 percent in 2003, the first full year that China was the largest export market for both South Korea and Taiwan. Globalization appears to have very much support in China. A research study by the Pew Center for the People & the Press in 2003 found that 90 percent of people surveyed in China felt that growing trade and business ties were "very good" or "somewhat good" for the country. China's emergence as an economic giant has not shown a considerable transformation into a high score in the index. Many of the indicators in the index are calculated on a per capita basis. Owing to its substantial population, China has struggled to look up its place in the ranking.

During our visit to China, Mr. Zhao Gancheng, Director of the Department of South Asia Studies and a senior fellow, spoke to me on July 25, 2006, at the Shanghai Institute for International Studies, which believes that China is making progress in coastal areas more rapidly as compared to inner areas. Chinese do not say China has any periphery or core areas, but they divide China into coastal, middle, and inner areas. It is again a gesture of keeping their separate identity on the part of the Chinese think tank.

China is kick-starting economic processes that foster Asian connectivity; China's heavy infrastructural investments from Afghanistan to Myanmar incorporate manpower trained by India and Japan; hence, Asian ties are not just being deepened to China but also to one another. Intra-Asian connectivity will increase on account of geopolitical rivalries, leading to the accelerated flow of inner Asian goods.[44]

Made in China is a popular slogan in the Chinese middle areas wherein different shopping plazas sales girls vocally say, "Be Chinese, buy Chinese." They believe in Chinese quality as they make different things in different grades to satisfy each segment of society, not only of their country but also of the world. It is trying to dominate the world economic market by making low-profile consumer goods without considering their pros and cons.

> "The economic results of China's reforms have been staggering. Between 1980 and 2000, the average person's income in China almost tripled, from $1,394 to $ 3,976. Some 170 million people have moved above the poverty line. Exports from the dynamic coastal provinces have been skyrocketed. Shenzen sold $17 million worth of goods in 1981; ten years later the figure was $ 5.9 billion; today it is over $ 30 billion. Foreign investment in these areas has surged."[45]

Amy Chua explains in her *World on Fire* gives a concept of "market-dominant minorities": these are ethnic minorities who, for widely varying reasons, tend under market conditions to dominate economically, often to a startling extent "indigenous" majorities around them. Many Chinese have migrated to Burma (Myanmar), Indonesia, the Philippines, Taiwan, Vietnam, and other Asian countries, including Pakistan, where they do their business efficiently and profitably. In some countries, China has dominated the local market in a way that irritates the indigenous businessman.

In Burma, many Chinese came from nearby Yunnan, had bought up identity papers of dead Burmans for only three hundred dollars, and became Burmese nationals in no time.[46]

"The Chinese have owned maximum business in Burma, "Only a tiny dying handful of Burman-owned establishments (mainly printing houses and cheroot factories) are left, dwarfed by the Chinese-built and Chinese-owned high-rise buildings around."[47] Besides that, several joint business ventures have reduced the number of other countries of Southeast Asia in economic domains as compared to China. For example, a deal between Shangri-La Hotel and LoHsing Han, "the Sino-Burmese chairman of the Asia World Conglomerate, and Sino-Malaysian tycoon Robert Kuok-have turned Mandalay and Rangoon into booming hubs for mainland Chinese and South Asian Chinese business networks."[48]

In this perspective, most of the Burmese think that China is looting a major amount of their land.[49] It is breeding hatred among local people against the "foreigners." Contrary to this, when one asks about this market domination in South East Asia, Chinese economic intelligentsia reply, "It is an exaggeration we are having good relations with our adjoining countries." If you ask the same intelligentsia about the market-dominant minorities in China in the form of MNCs-the Chinese prefer to have joint ventures with those MNCs and do not allow them to have any price hike without permission of the government. The Chinese are very careful about the monopoly of any MNCs in China. Even in this age of globalization, China has full control over its mobile companies. By the late 1990s, China has emerged as one of the world's largest auto markets and had succeeded to attract the inflows of capital, expertise, and technology from Western automakers. Presently, China is the largest auto producer in the world.[50]

To promote the idea of China Goes Global (CGG) President Jiang remarked, "In the long run to compete more effectively internationally, we must create a large number of large internationally cooperative enterprises and multinationals.... All enterprises that have the capability and the conditions, including SOEs as well as enterprises in other sectors, should boldly go global...though equal and mutually beneficial international cooperation.... I have thought about this matter for a long time, mainly for the sake of the future development of our country and the welfare of future generations of the Chinese nation."[51]

The Chinese economy is no more a secluded 'peasant-based economy of the Mao and early Deng Xiaoping eras. It has become an integral part of the 'Electronic Herd'[52] (It is a herd that does its business worldwide through computers, the internet, and MNCs) since the Chinese leadership knows that today, no country can live without this herd if any country tries to live without it she has to face the music ultimately.[53]

"The Electronic Herd is made up of all the faceless stock, bond, and currency traders sitting behind computer screens all over the globe, moving their money around from mutual funds to pension funds to emerging market funds, or trading on the internet from their basements."[54]

Golden Straitjacket[55] versus Gold Plated Jacket

Thomas L. Friedman believes that this age of globalization has its wearing in the form of a Golden Straitjacket that has to be put on by every country if it wishes to sustain itself in the community of nations.[56] This jacket has its golden rules: privatization, stable prices, downsizing, deregulation, free-market competition, the balance of payments, the balance of trade, FDI, elimination of corruption, and monopoly are such pieces interwoven to make this standard-size jacket for the whole world.[57] Therefore, whoever wears this jacket becomes part of the Western world system.

China intends to wear this jacket by making it at home as she always copies certain things at home and cheaply provides the same to the rest of the world. In the same way, China believes that this Golden Straitjacket can be prepared at home, making it a comfortable outfit. China has pragmatically prepared a 'gold plated jacket' which is a Golden Straitjacket for the West. It (the West) is making a fool of the rest by showing this Golden Straitjacket to the world as a real source of their economic development. All that glitters is not gold.

Therefore, China is befooling the West with the 'Gold Plated Jacket' for economic development. The Western Golden Straitjacket is only fit for the few, and more interestingly, it is put on by different countries according to their own need. Friedman writes,

> "Not every country puts on the Golden Straitjacket all the way some just go partway or a little at a time (India, Egypt), some put it on and take it off (Malaysia, Russia). Some try to tailor it to their specific culture and wear a few of the buttons unfastened (Germany, Japan, and France). Some think that they can resist their pinch altogether because they have a natural resource such as oil (Iran, Saudi Arabia). And some are so poor and isolated, with a government able to force people to accept being poor, that they can get away with dressing their

people, not in a Golden Straitjacket, but a plain old straitjacket (North Korea, Cuba, Sudan, Afghanistan)."[58]

The difference between China and the West is that China is making a fool of the West only, but the West is making a fool of the rest. It may be an oversimplification of China that she is making a fool of the West as the West may intentionally be giving way to China in world trade to penetrate and exchange its culture in a centrally controlled political system. The Golden Straitjacket suits only the West or its allies, not the rest. China does not force any other country to put on a Gold Plated Jacket.

Under the influence of the gold-plated jacket, more than five hundred top brands of the world are working in China. They are fighting with each other to capture the Chinese market. For example, in aerospace, Airbus and Boeing, Astra Zeneca, GlaxoSmithKline, Merck, and Pfizer in pharmaceuticals; BP, Exon, and Shell in oil and petrochemicals; Ericson, IBM, Nokia, and Siemens in information technology hardware; BMW, Ford, GM, Toyota, and VW in automobiles, Coca-Cola and Pepsi in soft drinks, Japan Tobacco, BAT and Philip Morris in tobacco, AIG, Allianz, Axa, CGNU and Prudential in insurance; Citigroup, Deutsche Bank, Credit Suisse, and JP Morgan Chase in banking; AOL-Time Warner, and News Corp in mass media are classic examples of such MNCs those are struggling hard for sustaining in Chinese economic market.[59]

Role of IFIs in China

China is a unique country with a successful economic development story without the role of Bretton Woods institutions (IMF, WB). It may be a blessing that these IFIs are not working actively in China; it may harm the Chinese economy as it undermined the economy of the Southeast Asian countries in the late 1990s. The fact is that Chinese leadership is very vigilant and did not give way to the IMF and the World Bank to play with the Chinese economy for the benefit of big powers. Contrary to this, China always gave respect to the IFIs not owing to their role in the Chinese political system but for having a moderate view of these institutions. China is not a hardliner country; it has different phases of relationships with international organizations.

Professor Wang Yizhou gives details of Chinese relations with international organizations in his edited document named Construction with Contradiction: in which the first phase started in 1949 and ended in 1970. During this period, China fought for its membership in the U.N. In the 1950s, it also applied for membership in different international organizations, like the International Civil Aviation Organization, IMF, International Labor Organization, World Health

Organization, World Meteorological Organization, etc., but failed to owe to the U.S. veto power being consistently used against China. The second phase 1971-78, gave China a real boost in the world community when she got membership in the UN and many other international Organizations. The third phase started in 1979 and is still in progress, it got membership of WTO after fifteen years of hard struggle.[60]

In the 1990s, almost all major players were "knocking on China's door," and it witnessed the arrival of a large number of automakers. In fact, during the same year, Western MNCs lobbied policymakers and industrial ministries. In 1993 alone, there were 65 high-profile meetings and visits of Western automakers to China.[61]

It is said that IFIs have assisted China in financial restructuring by introducing international standards and providing training to Chinese personnel in different domains. For example, China developed its external debt surveillance with the help of the World Bank. China also got technical assistance from the World Bank in developing five category-loan classification systems in the banking industry in early 2002.[62]

> "For China to implement its agreements with the World Trade Organization (WTO) the regime will have to force transparency, accountability, and market discipline across large swaths of the domestic economy. China's entry into the WTO is likely to be a slow but seismic change."[63]

Chinese leadership believes that there is no option to avoid globalization. This attitude is in accord with the understanding of globalization by the International Monetary Fund. As Eduardo Aninat, IMF Deputy Managing Director, noted, "China must make decisions that will determine how well it integrates further into the global system. There is no longer a question of whether to integrate, but only of how best to do so."[64] Appendix I is a detailed document of China's membership in the WTO and how it is embracing opportunities and facing challenges. (See Appendix I).

Economic globalization has caused a brain drain in China; since 1978, it is believed that 1.6 million people went overseas for education or job purposes but did not return home. They got married there or had permanent residence and nationalities. It has been noticed that only 275000 people came back home out of 1.6 million since 1978.[65]

BRI has accelerated China's outbound globalization to different regions. Most bilateral memorandums of understanding (MOUs) were signed with Central, South, and Southeast Asia. Comparing regional trends in 2010 and 2015 suggested that Central Asia's share revived to a modest 0.65 in 2015, and South Asia's share increased to 6.7 percent in 2015.[66]

Socio-Cultural Effects

China has long been under the influence of traditionalism that determines its future course of action, "the scope and level of its aspirations and the policies and strategies that are likely to be adopted to get it there."[67] In this perspective, the three periods are the most relevant first imperial period, which remained for more than two millenniums. The second period was of "foreign humiliation," which lasted until the twentieth century. The third period began with the communist revolution in China in 1949 and remained until the reform period of the 1970s.[68] These three periods describe the fortunes and misfortunes in China in different phases of history.[69]

China also made a cultural, civilizational, and institutional impact on its surrounding countries like Japan and Korea. Like the West, China did not impose its government institutions and culture upon its precincts, but it was adopted by surrounding countries voluntarily-who considered China "the most civilized, cultured and advanced nation on earth."[70] The Chinese intelligentsia believes that China should take the good aspects of Western Civilization without losing its own identity.[71]

Asian fashion models are also emerging on the global stage, gracing many Western fashion magazines and succeeding in earning a spot among the highest-paid models, such as Liu Wen from China. Moreover, Chinese film directors are highlighting numerous social issues and bringing local content to global screens. For example, Wang Bing confronted the issue of labor camps and minorities in his famous documentaries. China is not just opening new movie screens every day but also incorporates architectural environments along with 4D experiences for a global audience.[72]

China is shifting towards liberalism; in fact, it is copying Western countries in many aspects. For example, porn movie studios can be found operating next door to elementary schools; striped dancing in public parks, etc. These activities are common in China. Some scholars are apprehensive about the predicament of deteriorating morality in China.

It seems owing to some reasons that may be explained first, China has misled people about the Western lifestyle. Western life is misunderstood in China as promiscuity and nightclubs everywhere. People feel that if they go to those clubs and dance, they will be looking as developed as the Western world. It is not so simple. By eating McDonald's burgers and drinking Coke, dancing in clubs cannot make anyone a Westerner. It is a false imitation of misunderstood Western values.

Secondly, the present Chinese government is giving people freedom without considering its consequences. Thirdly, China is not afraid of losing its traditional values in the wake of modernization. She believes that to play an active role in the world political economy, it has to adopt certain Western ways of living. Fourthly, ideologically, China seems very pathetic as it has had Confucian ideology for 2000 years (also in Japan and Korea), but now it is repudiated.[73]

The negative effects of globalization in China can be seen in cultural terms. This has brought in information and products on the one hand and affected the culture on the other. For example, in food, drinks, music, movies, etc., the Chinese are becoming very fond of the West in entertainment. KFC and McDonald's can be found in most cities in China, where people stand in queues to enjoy Western-origin food, but the Chinese taste fast food.

Young boys and girls are free to live together independently, but unlike the West, they do not believe in short-term and a long-term relationship but in perfect marriages. The divorce rate, extramarital relations, and other crimes like snatching mobile phones, street robbery, and looting taxi drivers have grown. Most taxi drivers have a fence around the driving seat in China. They have the fence owing to increasing robbery cases in China.

World Olympics 2022 will be held in China, another effort by the West to penetrate the Chinese political system through its cultural and social system. The question is how Chinese leadership will face this challenge successfully. It seems quite evident that China was mentally prepared for transformation after 1979, and it easily swallowed the global forces that emerged after the 1990s collapse of communism. Therefore, it may be successful in 2008, but doubts remain intact owing to social and cultural changes in China where people are more open and victims of acculturation for the last quarter of the century.

One other aspect that can also be considered very important is that MNCs are taking a heavy toll on environmental degradation in China. The problem is not those companies polluting the environment but that the guilty party can get away without much punishment.[74]

People are very much satisfied with the ongoing progress in China. Their Isothymia, (to consider himself equal to others) part of the soul is more dominant. In Chinese leaders, Isothymia cum Megalothymia (to consider himself superior to others) are both dominant. They are no longer dominant with the Microthymia part of the soul (to consider themselves inferior to others).[75] Now, we look into the fact that globalization is taking a heavy toll on the Chinese environment.

Globalization and its Impact on the Chinese Environment

Despite populist arguments, President Jiang Zemin, Premier Zhu Rongji, Minister Long Yongtu, and other Chinese leadership have a consensus on one point that globalization could not be reversed.[76] China is making headway, leaps and bounds. Globalization has caused economic growth in China, along with polluting the environment. It is a serious threat to Chinese people in the future. For a sustainable and disease-free environment, China has to enact pragmatic laws for MNCs that could stop them from deteriorating the environment.

Chinese coastal areas are the worst for marine life in China and are also a menace for its adjoining territories like Taiwan and Kinmen Island. "Bottles, plastic bags, rags and effluent from China is washing up on the otherwise pristine beaches of the Taiwan-controlled, sub-tropical island of Kinmen, better known in the West as Quemoy."[77] Another prosperous coastal city of China, Xiamen, is also causing environmental pollution due to its garbage-ridden currents, which destroy marine life in Taiwan.[78] Chinese garbage is not only disturbing Taiwan but also polluting seawater and polluting the air in Japan, Hong Kong, and South Korea.[79]China seems apathetic towards the polluted environment. It has already made a council named as China Council for International Cooperation on Environment and Development but it is not pragmatic in fighting against environmental pollution in China. There are hundreds of local and foreign companies, manufacturing consumer goods in China.

It is not only China that is facing environmental pollution in the wake of industrialization and economic growth but also other countries like America, India, and Japan are also facing the same dilemma.

However, they are cooperating for keeping this planet healthy. First, we look at the following graph that gives us a clear picture that how much carbon dioxide is being emitted by these economically prosperous countries.

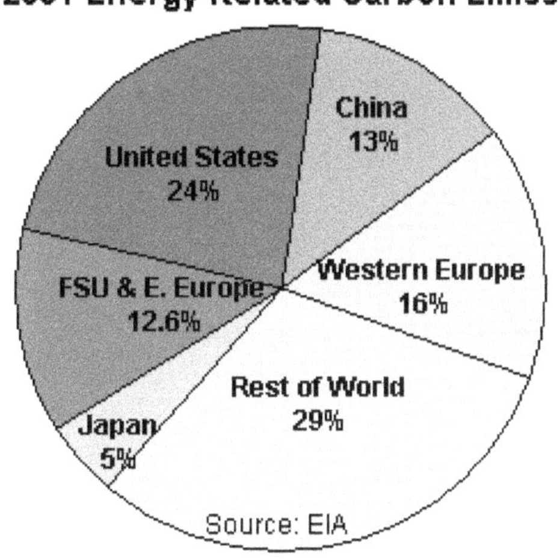

Source: http://www.eia.doe.gov/emeu/cabs/chinaenv.html.Website visited on 09-05-07.

The above-shown graph categorically gives an idea that in 2001, China, with 13% emission of carbon dioxide, was the second largest after the U.S. It is predicted that by 2025, its emission of carbon dioxide will reach up to 18%.[80] China is doing its best to curtail the burning of coal as much as possible. "China has introduced bold initiatives to cut back on coal use. To encourage a switch to cleaner-burning fuels, the government has introduced a tax on high-sulfur coals, and in Beijing, officials aiming to phase out coal from the city center have established 40 "coal-free zones" and have made plans to construct natural gas pipelines."[81]

Hardware/Software versus Humanware[82]

China is not facing today the problem of hardware or software but "Humanware."[83] After the communist revolution in China in 1949, intellectual or educated people started leaving the country for better freedom of life. In the twenty-first century, China needs a strong social system to sustain itself successfully in the world community.

China urges to get its skilled, Western-educated social capital back in the native land to improve the standards of social life in all interconnected domains like social, political, and economic. It is only possible when the Chinese government introduces new reforms and incentives to attract its educated elite. Without that, 'Humanware' China cannot think to invest in high-tech labor products.[84]

It has two plans to attain its targets. First, the Chinese government is ready to make educational reforms to create more pragmatic and workable social capital. Second, China needs its engineers and scientists back home who have gone to a different industrialized world. First, it was criticized that those educated people might come up with modern ideas like democracy that could harm the Chinese system, but China welcomes them for its advantage, calling them 'turtles' as they tend to return to their birthplace.[85]

The Qinghai-Tibet Railway is an engineering accomplishment that passes through the permafrost region at a height of almost 4,000 meters. As soon as this 1,956-kilometer route begins at the end of this year, it will enhance China's strategic capability near the Sino-Indian border and assist in the development of Tibet. Regional unevenness is also surmounted through other projects like the South-to-North water transport project and the West-to-East gas pipeline project. Similarly, the Three Gorges is the leading multi-use project in the world. Billed as China's biggest construction since the Great Wall, this energy dinosaur, once fully commissioned in 2009, will generate an additional 11 percent of China's installed electricity capacity.[86]

Beijing and Shanghai areas developed as any Western city in terms of urban road and rail network and social life. The forthcoming Shanghai World Financial

Centre, with a height of 492 meters, will be taller than Petronas Towers in Kuala Lumpur. China is making its bullet trains and runs a vast network of expressways. Hong Kong's Chek Lap Kok airport is most likely the most modern in design.

Countries are generally viewed first by differences based on their political systems but surprisingly, India supports top-down economic reforms of China. Sociopolitical and cultural divergence does not preclude cross-border learning in this globalized era. Unlike democratic India, the average Chinese citizen has a better standard of living under the communist system.[87]

All these aspects show that China intends to achieve 'comprehensive national power.' In this pretext, China is also making good progress in its latent power. China's 'poverty reduction' program is a considerable achievement, dropping its poor people to 200 million. China is also trying to eliminate rising regional inequality. It has commenced the 'Western development project' and 'Northeast revival' to build up these regions at par with coastal China.[88]

Dr. Bhartendu explains that China has also flourished in information technology (IT) and is considered a nucleus of the IT world. It is the principal exporter of IT goods, including mobile phones, notebooks, personal computers, and digital cameras. Shanghai is the world's leading port after leaving behind Singapore and has come out as the third largest trading nation ($1.4 trillion in 2005), running massive trade surpluses with the U.S. and EU. CGG is attributed as an "independent and proactive globalization strategy. "that guarantees government participation in global competition."[89] Chinese companies are making rapid headway and overcoming other foreign investors, including U.S. companies. China is a leading country in attracting FDI and rising as a huge global consumer market. We conducted in-depth interviews with the Chinese intelligentsia to study China in this age of globalization empirically. See Appendix II, III, and IV for in-depth interviews with Chinese political, economic, and military intelligentsia.

Conclusions drawn from In-depth Interviews with Chinese Intelligentsia

After having a closer look into the expression of these interviews and matching it with their society during the visit to China, it seems that Chinese economic development is remarkable, and it is not only accepted in China but the world over. Regarding the political aspect, the Chinese have their system but overestimate the communist party. Even having a difference in their views all the interviewers supported and opposed their government at the same time. It shows their dissatisfaction with the present political system in China.

The most affected part of Globalization is the Chinese social system. In China, in the wake of globalization, the family system is affected very deeply; the divorce rate has increased and is increasing daily.

Second, the Chinese social system is semi-Western, but the Chinese young generation is going to nightclubs and bars, dancing with dangling lights, and taking alcohol without care with their partners. They have nightclubs like Baby Face, Far Away, Destination, etc.

Young girls and boys are allowed to have dates and open kissing in bazaars and plazas. It is not yet as much as it may be in Europe or the West, but they are getting Western very quickly. They cannot recognize Madonna as a popular singer even though they do not know what she sings, but dancing to English music and having fun. Like other societies, the Chinese are very concerned about their interests only.

They have developed big shopping plazas with escalators, believing customers should be treated well until they want to buy. After buying, they do not need care and treatment, as there are no escalators for getting down after shopping on the fifth or sixth floor. Although a few big plazas have both up-going and downward escalators yet, whatever we say about them, it is true that they have made a difference in the world economic community.

Chinese media has also adopted very much of the style of the West. But its TV channels are all in Chinese language; few news bulletins are in English, like World Wide Watch on CCTV International. In China, BTV, CCTV, and CETV are major channels; along with them, HEBTV, HLJTV, NNTV, SDETV, TJTV, XZTV, and many others having Chinese names are also contributing a lot in entertaining, educating, and creating awareness among people. All these channels more or less have the same style of presentation and entertainment as TV channels have in Asia and the West. The difference lies in their approach. In Asia and the West, media is used mostly for commercial purposes, and in China, along with commercial purposes, it is also used for the propagation of the communist party and the government.

Globalization has positively impacted the economic domain of China but negatively in the political and social domains. It is among the first five nations of the world that have economic prosperity. It is all because Chinese individuals actively participate in and develop the system with sweat. They do not need any sweatshops in China. It is a commitment on the part of the people; unless it is there, they will progress.

Socially, globalization hurts China. China is really at stake. It is very difficult to say why they are adopting Western values so rapidly without having any language understanding. English is still far from Chinese people. Even the intellectuals of China cannot effectively communicate it (in English). It looks like China is still unwilling to learn more about English. The people in China are trying to learn it to stand in the world community. They do not feel proud to be good at English.

China's rise as a magnanimous power may be acceptable or even welcomed. China's outward investment and lending are shaped by its prioritization for internal growth.[90] Politically, globalization could make a difference in China. In the political field, it seems they are very much satisfied and unwilling to have any change but are making some changes to absorb the external shocks of globalization. Hence, if the Chinese became aware ever that their political system also needs their push it may start after one or two decades. This political strife may be for democracy or any other system that can emerge at any time in the future.

More than ninety percent of signboards are in the Chinese language, and the rest, ten percent, are translated into English owing to the Chinese's advantage, as all translated signboards belong to tourism, restaurants, and Banks. Therefore, it was necessary to get the maximum benefit. It is not only an age of globalization but also an age of commercialization.

Corruption is deep-rooted in China. It exists from the bottom to the top echelons of the Chinese ruling party and other segments of society. Taxi drivers, extraordinary businessmen, peons, and high officials are mostly corrupt.

Besides all disparities, the Chinese economy is rising as everyone contributing to China in response to the government is supporting its individuals in financial crises. For example, an old person is paid 2000 Yuan by the government for living a healthy, satisfying life in China. Common people are supported by sending their children to schools. The government gives a fee for two children in each family. That is why the role of the individual in the development of the Chinese economy is very much active. Even when Sino-American relations deteriorated in the late 1990s on account of the U.S.' accidental bombing of the Chinese embassy, the diaspora community helped China to maintain the liberalization trend.[91]

China's Kuafu Mission is going to probe the Sun. it is China's first-ever space mission that will be completed in 2012. It is named after Kuafu, who tried to catch the sun but failed. It shows that China is also struggling to make headway in high technology and space. Chinese lunar exploration project is also under process, again showing Chinese development in all sectors owing to the age of globalization.

Future of China

"The only thing certain about China is uncertainty."[92] The following table predicts a very idealist form for the Chinese and a pessimistic one for Americans.

Import growth	Export Growth 12%	Export Growth 25%	Export Growth 33%
20%	-$330	-$ 290	-$ 252
15%	-$ 246	-$ 205	-$ 167
10%	-$ 178	-$ 138	-$ 100
7%	-$ 144	-$ 104	-$ 66

Source: Oded Shenkar, *The Chinese Century*, 170.

This table shows a projected change in the U.S. trade deficit with China by 2008 (in billions of dollars). China plays a major role in international and regional level organizations. G7, G8, G22, Shanghai 5, and Shanghai Cooperation Organization, (SCO), ASEAN, and Asia-Pacific Economic Cooperation are all classic examples of Chinese increasing participation in the world community. China is very much alert as far as its concerns are concerned. China is promoting anti-terrorism, anti-extremism, and increased cooperation.

The SCO "established in June 2001 to capitalize on earlier joint confidence-building efforts among China, Russia, Kazakhstan, Tajikistan, Kyrgyzstan, and Uzbekistan, is designed to achieve a more institutionalized form of cooperation on issues ranging from antiterrorism to trade. Chinese leaders now hail the SCO as a model of regional cooperation that enhances collective security for the participants while not threatening any outside party."[93]

Chinese future is correlated with the intensity of desire for development on the part of leadership and the common individual. Recently, the Chinese state has rolled out anti-poverty programs by allocating more budget for social welfare. Moreover, in light of President Xi's pledge to eliminate poverty by 2030, the state is ensuring stable revenue sources. [94] As long as both segments of society back each other for the welfare of the whole of China, it keeps on flourishing. China will decline as soon as that linkage between leaders and the leaders breaks away.

We can say that Ibn-i-Khuldoon's philosophy of 'Asbiyya' and 'Phases of State' seems to be in action. He explains the sense of oneness or integration (Asbiyya) takes a state towards the culmination of progress; leaders and the led work together, and then, with time, they become lethargic and face downward progress.

After having a close look at globalization and its impact on China, we proceed towards our fourth chapter, which will explain how India is another power of the region with a different form of government, economy, and culture, behaves in this age of globalization.

Endnotes

1 Min Ye, Diasporas and Foreign Direct Investment in China and India: Cambridge University Press, 2014, 08.

2 Daniel Lerner, *The Passing Of Traditional Society*, Glencoe, III, Free Press, 1958, 438. Cited in Samuel P. Huntington, *Political Order in Changing Societies,* London: Yale University Press, 1968, 32-33.

3 Ibid.

4 Samuel P. Huntington, *Political Order in Changing Societies,* London: Yale University Press, 1968, 32-33.

5 Ibid.

6 Parag Khanna, *THE FUTURE IS ASIAN: Commerce, Conflict, and Culture in the 21st Century*: Simon & Schuster, 2019, 71.

7 Robert A. Dahl, *Who Governs?* New Haven, Yale University Press, 1961, 85-86. Cited in Huntington, *Political Order,*33.

8 Min Ye, *The Belt Road and Beyond: State-Mobilized Globalization in China: 1998-2018*: Cambridge University Press, 2020,217.

9 Huntington, *Political Order,* 33.

10 Karl W. Deutsch, "Social Mobilization and Political Development," *American Political Science Review,* 55 (September 1961), 494.

11 Huntington, *Political Order,* 34.

12 Ibid.

13 Ibid., 35.

14 Ibid., 37-38.

15 Parag Khanna, *THE FUTURE IS ASIAN: Commerce, Conflict, and Culture in the 21st Century*: Simon & Schuster, 2019, 139.

16Huntington uses traditional (developed) societies and transitional (developing) societies in his book *Political Order in Changing Societies.* In this thesis, we are using these terms to denote developing and developed countries for our purpose.

17 Min Ye, *Diasporas and Foreign Direct Investment in China and India*: Cambridge University Press, 2014, 117.

18Minxin Pei, "The Dark Side of China," *Foreign Policy Journal*, March/April, 2006. http://www.foreignpolicy.com/story/cms.php?story_id=3373&page=3 visited on 02-03-06.

19 Ibid.

20 Peter Nolan, *Transforming China: Globalization, Transition and Development,* London: Anthem Press, 2004, 77.

21²1 Ibid., 79-80.

22 Ibid., 81.

23 Ibid., 45.

24 Deng Xiaoping, "Uphold the Four Cardinal Principles," Excerpts, http://www.wellesley.edu/Polisci/wj/China/Deng/principles.htm, Visited on 15-03-2006.

25 Oded Shenkar, *The Chinese Century: The Rising Chinese Economy and Its Impact on the Global Economy, the Balance of Power, and Your Job,* Pennsylvania: Wharton School Publishing, 2005, 34.

26 Nolan, *Transforming China,* 81.

27 Ibid.

28 Ibid., 90.

29 Ibid., 78.

30 Fareed Zakaria, The *Future of Freedom: Illiberal Democracy Home and Abroad,* New York: W.W. Norton & Company, 2004, 81.

31 Ibid.

32 *Dawn,* June 30, 2007.

33 Thomas L. Friedman, *Understanding Globalization: The Lexus and The Olive Tree,* New York: Anchor Books, INC., 1999, 169.

34 Ibid.

35 Ibid., 258.

36 Ibid.

37 http://www.licenseenews.com/news/news276.html, Visited on 10-09-06.

38 http://www.newstarget.com/000965.html, Visited on 10-09-06

39 Parag Khanna, *THE FUTURE IS ASIAN: Commerce, Conflict, and Culture in the 21st Century:* Simon & Schuster, 2019, 221-290.

40 Parag Khanna, *THE FUTURE IS ASIAN: Commerce, Conflict, and Culture in the 21st Century:* Simon & Schuster, 2019, 221-222.

41 Xuewu Gu, *China and its Reactions to Globalization,* http://www.bpb.de/files/E4SM4X.pdf, visited on 16-03-06.

42 Oded Shenkar, *The Chinese Century,* 2.

43 Parag Khanna, *THE FUTURE IS ASIAN: Commerce, Conflict, and Culture in the 21st Century:* Simon & Schuster, 2019, 24.

44 Parag Khanna, *THE FUTURE IS ASIAN: Commerce, Conflict, and Culture in the 21st Century:* Simon & Schuster, 2019, 113.

45 Zakaria, *The Future of Freedom,* 82.

46 Amy Chua, *World on Fire,* New York: Anchor Books, inc., 2003, 24.

47 Ibid., 25.

48 Ibid.

49 Ibid., 30.

50 Min Ye, *Diasporas and Foreign Direct Investment in China and India:* Cambridge

University Press, 2014, 171.

51 Min Ye, *The Belt Road and Beyond: State-Mobilized Globalization in China: 1998-2018*: Cambridge University Press, 2020,41.

52 Friedman, *Understanding Globalization,* 259.

53 Ibid., 257.

54 Ibid., 109.

55 Ibid.,101.

56 Ibid., 104.

57 Ibid., 105.

58 Ibid., 108.

59 Peter Nolan, *Transforming China,* 239.

60 Wang Yizhou, ed., *Construction with Contradiction,* Beijing: China Development Publishing House, 2003.

61 Min Ye, *Diasporas and Foreign Direct Investment in China and India*: Cambridge University Press, 2014, 165.

62 http://www.g7.utoronto.ca/g20/20030831_cs_chi.pdf#search=%22the%20role%20of%20IFIs%20in%20China%22, visited on 14-09-06.

63 Zakaria, *The Future of Freedom,* 82.

64 Eduardo Aninat, China, Globalization, and the IMF, Speech on the Foundation for Globalization Cooperation's Second Globalization Forum, Sanya City, China, January 2001. (http://www.imf.org/external/np/speeches/2001/01140.html, 21/06/2001).

65 *Dawn* Lahore, June 3, 2007, 14

66 Min Ye, *The Belt Road and Beyond: State-Mobilized Globalization in China: 1998-2018*: Cambridge University Press, 2020,112.

67 Oded Shenkar, *The Chinese Century,* 25.

68 Ibid.

69 Ibid., 26.

70 Ibid., 29.

71 Ibid., 31.

72 Parag Khanna, *THE FUTURE IS ASIAN: Commerce, Conflict, and Culture in the 21st Century*: Simon & Schuster, 2019, 310-311.

73 http://www.peacehall.com/news/gb/english/2005/03/200503201230.shtml, visited on 27-02-06.

74 Ibid.

75 For details, see my M. Phil Thesis, *Globalization and its Impact on Pakistan Politics 1990-2000.*

76 Min Ye, *The Belt Road and Beyond: State-Mobilized Globalization in China: 1998-2018*: Cambridge University Press, 2020,90.

77   http://www.planetark.com/avantgo/dailynewsstory.cfm?newsid=40447.   Website visited on 01-05-07.

78 Ibid.

79 Ibid.

80 http://www.eia.doe.gov/emeu/cabs/chinaenv.html. Website visited on 09-05-07.

81 Ibid.

82 Oded Shenkar, *The Chinese Century*, 72.

83 Ibid.

84 Ibid.

85 Ibid., 75.

86 Dr Bhartendu Kumar Singh, China: Great Power, Grand Projects, http://www.ipcs. org/whatsNewArticle1.jsp? action=showView&kValue=1941&status=article&mod=b. Website visited on 06-04-06.

87 Parag Khanna, *THE FUTURE IS ASIAN: Commerce, Conflict, and Culture in the 21st Century*: Simon & Schuster, 2019, 275.

88 Ibid.

89 Min Ye, *The Belt Road and Beyond: State-Mobilized Globalization in China: 1998-2018*: Cambridge University Press, 2020,87.

90 Min Ye, *The Belt Road, and Beyond: State-Mobilized Globalization in China: 1998-2018*: Cambridge University Press, 2020,143.

91 Min Ye, *Diasporas and Foreign Direct Investment in China and India*: Cambridge University Press, 2014, 96.

92 Ibid., 169.

93 Yong Deng and Thomas G. Moore, China Views Globalization: Toward a New Great-Power Politics? *The Washington Quarterly*, vol. 117, summer 2004, visited on http:// yaleglobal.yale.edu/about/pdfs/china_views.pdf visited on 16-03-06.

94 Min Ye, *The Belt Road and Beyond: State-Mobilized Globalization in China: 1998-2018*: Cambridge University Press, 2020,31.

Chapter 3. India and Globalization: Attributes

India is the second-largest country in the world by population after China. Its second-largest economic market has also made India more attractive to the developed world. In the twenty-first century, India has developed itself so that its poverty remains under the influence of regional power status.

India is a plural state with many religions, languages, cultures, and caste systems. It is a heterogeneous state with a warm climate. In this age of globalization, India plays a significant role in world politics. Its film industry is one of the biggest industries in the world.

Being a consociational (a grouping of political parties or pressure groups within a region or country that work together to share power)[1] state, India claims itself to be a secular country, but these claims went vain after incidents like Khalistan, Babri Mosque, Hyderabad Muslim killings, and setting fire in one of the Christian temples in India.

According to Fareed Zakaria,

> "India is a genuinely free and freewheeling society. But looking under the cover of Indian democracy, one sees a more complex and troubling reality. In recent decades, India has become quite different from the picture in the hearts of its admirers. Considering the realities mentioned above, it seems to be a less democratic state, but in so many important ways, it has become more democratic, but it has become less tolerant, less secular, less law-abiding, and less liberal…"[2]

Prime Minister Modi has realized that India has been subjected to political devolution, so its current existence is less than the sum of its parts. Tracing back to independence, India had only fourteen provinces, but further fragmentation divided it into twenty-nine provinces. The federally structured National Institution for Transforming India (NITI) has also replaced the old Planning Commission to promote economic transformations. Besides economic reforms, the Indian Prime Minister is following Lee Kuan Yew to tackle corruption in the country.[3]

Indian Barbarianism was at its peak when Indira Gandhi launched state terrorism against the Sikh community in 1984 under P.V. Narasimha Rao, who was the home minister at that time. The Babri mosque debacle in 1992 and the Muslim riots in 1993 occurred under the supervision of Dr. Manmohan Singh. The Gujarat massacre in 2002 was another sad aspect of Indian so-called secularism. The subjective attitude of the government allowed extremist elements to kill Sikhs in 1984 and Muslims in 1992 and 2002.[4]

India is playing very tactfully in international politics, as the West does not criticize India for its undemocratic attitude towards non-Hindu communities. India's economic market seems to allow it to do whatever it wishes. Owing to its enormous, lucrative economic market, India is taking advantage of globalization and boosting its economy. However, India is not as prosperous as China in the twenty-first century. Now onward, we try to see how India grapples with its affairs in the age of globalization.

Globalization and Its Impact on:

India's Political Placement

Politically, India is a secular and democratic country in the World Community. Its former president, Dr. Abulkalam, came from the Muslim community. Therefore, its claim as a secular country gives it credibility. However, incidents of Babri Mosque, Hyderabad, and setting ablaze Christian temple expose India's religiously biased country. It has successfully diluted all wrong impressions in the community of nations.

India's Political Placement in the Past

"The world's largest democracy" got a chance to develop its political institutions with democratic norms owing to its leadership that stayed longer than Pakistan after the partition of the subcontinent in 1947. India never experienced 'praetorianism' due to its developed political institution. Interestingly, authoritarianism had remained a characteristic of the Indian political system through the political elite. Dynastic politics played an essential role in the authoritative attributes of the Indian region.

Nehru and Gandhi's families had consistently inducted their representatives in different governments. It always kept the Indian political system in the traditional and inherited outfit. Nehru ruled not to govern India from 1947 to 1964. He once said he was "the last Englishman to rule India."[5] Even when holding fair elections in India, Congress achieved a two-thirds majority at all state levels.[6] Therefore, it was in favor of the Indian political system that it established its political institutions on solid lines. India has had a multi-party system since its independence, but it always observed the autocracy of one party, which was Congress. This autocracy was sustained until Rajeev Gandhi. However, the popularity of the Congress party came into question after Indira Gandhi's policies of nationalization put an end to the rights of Indian princes.[7] It created a vacuum in India that was filled by the Bhartiya Janata Party based on Hindu fundamentalism, making India "more democratic" but "less liberal."[8]

Comparing the pre-reform period of China and India reveals that specific political and economic conditions perplexed their FDI liberalization. First, large populations and territories contributed to cheap land and labor. Poor infrastructure and pathetic living conditions failed to attract Westerners. Socialism dominated after the independence. However, Maoism was more extreme than Nehru's political system. Additionally, fear of foreign imposition fostered ideological aversion, too. Despite similar contexts in China and India, economic transitions vary. Unlike India, FDI had played a more vital role in China.[9]

It shows that the Indian civil political elite gave birth to autocracy and authoritarianism. It is regrettable to say that Indian urban leaders like Jawaharlal Nehru, Indra Gandhi, and Rajeev Gandhi could not balance states living in the core and states located on the periphery. Hence, Indian democracy always lacked a link between leaders and the led. That missing link enhanced specific horizontal and vertical cleavages in India regarding linguistic, parochial, and ethnic in the first place and a lacuna between haves and have-nots in the second place. Kishwar, a senior fellow at the Centre for the Study of Developing Societies in Delhi, writes, "The political parties who came to power after India achieved independence played an active role in fragmenting our society by pitching various groups against each other and pushed narrow, partisan and often dangerous agendas."[10] It dissatisfied the masses, and uncertainty gave rise to political instability that peaked in India in the last decade of the twentieth century. The matter of fact is that no society can flourish smoothly with lopsided development. It shows that distributive capability is in a state of abeyance. It promotes the 'migration of dreams' and 'relative deprivation among masses.'

From December 2, 1989, to November 28, 1997, there have been six prime ministers in India. Shri Vishwanath Pratap Singh, Shri Chandra Shekhar, Shri P.V. Narasimha Rao, Shri Atal Behari Vajpayee, Shri H. D. Deve Gowda, and Shri Inder Kumar Gujral were the prime ministers who came into power one after the other.

India's Political Placement at Present

From 1947 to 2024, Indian civil governments had fourteen prime ministers as compared to Pakistan's military cum civilian governments had twenty-three prime ministers in the same era. It shows that only political institutions can ensure political stability when the leadership efficiently utilizes the system's capabilities. Otherwise, civilian government can destroy the political system more quickly than any other form of government.

Here are some views shared by Sunil Khilnani[11] in India as a bridging power, a persistent idea of India's place in the community of nations as a significant regional power. He is currently a professor of politics and director of South Asia

Studies at the Paul H. Nitze School of Advanced International Studies, the Johns Hopkins University, in Washington, DC. In India, intellectuals such as Tagore, Gandhi, and Nehru have condemned hidebound attitudes on the part of the Indian government and always supported global Indian obligations.

It has been very much in the news that India will be a 'superpower' by 2020. India is going to have a 'silent revolution based on the principles of democracy, economic growth, and political participation of the people that are making India a country of the new look. The emergence of hybrid technical-professional academies has accommodated the Indian youth bulge and middle class. Numerous industrial skills are being taught online to train this cohort for the local and global market. [12]

Sunil also explains that India has to work hard to sustain itself with the pace of globalization and utilize all its resources to the best of its ability. It includes a consistent economic growth rate with absolute interdependence that will augment India economically but not deprive it of observing full sovereignty as China did comprehensively. India has to be clear about its goals in international politics without any ambiguity that should be pursued accordingly. Today's world order has changed entirely. After the disintegration of the Soviet Union, change can be seen in the West, which came closer to defending itself against external influence; "in David Calleo's phrase, 'new age of geopolitical anxiety.'" The second change is all about the effects of the collapse of Arab nationalism replaced by the so-called Islamic extremism that is being felt in Europe, the U.S., Asia, and Africa. The third concerns China's rise as an economic giant and India's search to find its place as a significant global player.

According to Robert Kaplan, the new Silk Road will retain China's dominance. Tom Miller predicts that global power will shift from Anglo-Saxon capitals to Beijing. Strategic observers from Central, South, and Southeast Asia are also concerned about China's expansionism. Contrary to other preceding foreign policies, China is also outspoken in promoting BRI's global vision.[13]

Consequently, this world is jungle-like, where most countries make policies for their defense and security but expose themselves as more democratic, a universal friend of peace and human rights, where the state and market are our driving forces. In this uni-multipolar world, India looks quizzical about securing a lucrative position.

The preponderance of the U.S. in world politics has been a matter of grave concern with India. Therefore, its new role in world politics based on attaining a permanent seat in the Security Council of the U.N. has forced India to keep close relations with the U.S. for the last five years.

India and the U.S. both intend to make relations based on bilateralism. The Bush government considered India a strategic friend and urged it to have smooth relations with the same on sound grounds. As Sunil mentioned in his article above, "The Bush administration is interested in India's strategic potential for U.S. interests: as it stated in the 'National Security Strategy' (2002), 'today we start with a view of India as a growing world power with which we have common strategic interests."

It is a vocal statement by America for a country in the subcontinent because of its strategic and market-oriented state of affairs. America never accepted India as a genuine nuclear power but now finds advantages in nuclear India. Today, the U.S. is more concentrated on the "volatile crescent that stretches from Palestine to Indonesia - and to the presence that looms over this geographical curve, China," writes Sunil in his article. The U.S. is determined to check the 'volatile crescent' and contain China as a regional and a global power with the assistance of India.

In the contemporary age of Asianization, Asia is rising as a powerful region to shape the United States more than the contrary. Expansion of local currency borrowing and regional trade is weakening the dollar's value, U.S. markets, and the United States' overall financial position. On the one hand, the United States' strategic influence is declining in the region, while on the other hand, it is troubled because of increased economic dependence on Asia.[14]

In this increasingly interconnected world, the state with the power of adjustability according to international rules can play its role and take the fruits of globalization. A state with no such capability will be nowhere in the community of nations. Sunil rightly said that "the elements of power are now more diffusely spread, shared, and even entangled. Thus, small, relatively powerless states (or non-state actors) can damage more powerful states. Even the U.S. finds itself in this paradoxical position: at once invincible, and yet vulnerable."

That vulnerability does not lie in the acts of extremism. In the modern world, all centers of power, including America, Canada, China, the European Union, Japan, and India, are looking for lucrative markets for their goods, services, capital, and people "to sustain their momentum and fund its insatiable consumption." It is evident that only developing economies can sustain themselves in the present-day world politics of competing America and its allies. Both China and India can easily adjust themselves to this competition.

India wishes for an influential role in world politics where China as its counterpart exists and their interests conflict with each other. These dichotomies will exist and sharpen in the twenty-first century, taking on new and complex forms. In the twentieth century, neither China nor India were as influential as now. In the twenty-first century, they will be relatively affluent states with relatively poor populations having high national wealth but low per capita income. Consequently, there is a threat to both countries of internal tensions that may ultimately endanger the international community.

Sunil writes,

> "In the face of these persisting conflicts of interest, what common language of dialogue and persuasion can there be between the contending powers? This is a crucial question both for those who currently dominate the international order and for those who aspire to have an active role in it. They need to find a way of structuring conflicts of interest that does not break apart the international order. A breakdown can come from either end, from the powerless as much as the powerful. We have seen what Osama or Saddam can do."

Political trends keep changing in this age of globalization and have impacted the world. The modern world has seen that traditional power politics differs from contemporary power politics. For instance, in 1998, both China and the U.S. were against the Indian nuclear detonation. Today, India and the U.S. are worried about China's role in nuclear cooperation with North Korea and Pakistan. Such power politics does not create strong alliances in world politics. Hence, the present scenario suits India better than the U.S.

In the twenty-first century, regionalism is emerging as a strong force and regional integrating blocs can be considered a counter-current to the so-called modern cliché of globalization. Asia is divided into three regional integrated blocs: Asia, South East Asia, and South Asia, having different cultures and ideologies. They believe in interdependence, not dependentia. India is working hard to integrate regional blocs. Sunil explains that in the following words:

> "Regional institutions, such as the Asian Development Bank (India was a founding member, China joined in 1986), APEC (India is not yet a member), and ASEAN (India is a partner, though not yet a member), are gaining new relevance and new ones will need to be invented. China has been reluctant to recognize India as an 'Asian' country and has resisted Indian efforts to join such organizations."

However, India can sustain a strong position in world politics through genuine traits of liberal constitutional democracy. Sunil emphasizes that

> "Today, we live in a world where what has been called the 'battle of ideas, as well as the clash of images, is a crucial terrain of action. In the middle decades of the twentieth century, India projected a clear image of what it stood for while freely critical of the West; it firmly embraced shared enlightenment and modernist principles."

He further gives two examples in this respect for the contradicting nature of the Indian political system. In the first place, ".... 'Bangalore' and 'Gujarat': a choice between 'Brand Software' and 'Brand Saffron'; the promise of Bangalore and the threat of Gujarat." India must be careful about images that can distort Indian political legitimacy in world politics.

The second example is about Gujarat giving an expression that economic growth is linked with extremism ".... mainly when such growth occurs within an already complex society that possesses many potential lines of cleavage.

Indian diasporas in informatics were not comprised of dominant investors. Instead, they integrated the domestic market with global demand through working in Western companies. These diasporas also facilitated the entry of Western MNCs through channeling capital and technology in India. Additionally, the diaspora's knowledge helped share the needs, strengths, and demands of American and Indian markets, bringing the business partners together.[15]

Globalization has made a very positive impact on the Indian political system in that it has assimilated other communities successfully into its realm, especially Muslims. Bordering Bangladesh and Pakistan, India is the second-largest Muslim country in the world, with a liberal-democratic order. After the 9/11 incident, most parts of the world looked down upon Muslims. Still, India took them in confidence and amalgamated their identity into a national whole, and if it goes on. It will be a bizarre kind of relationship, and the world can take guidance from it on how other ideologies can be part of the system for peaceful coexistence.

Indian leadership thinks that dichotomy in the system may enhance unity and strength. Mr. Manmohan Singh said in his speech in New Delhi (5 November 2004) that India should observe democratic principles for setting an example as a role model for the developing world.

Although general elections have been a constant feature of the Indian political system, they did not ensure political freedom in India. Political freedom can only be enjoyed when there is economic freedom. "Political freedom has thus been understood in a very narrow sense of free and fair elections, right to representation in political institutions and decentralization of decision-making in civic affairs through devolution of powers to state governments, *Zila parishads and gram panchayats.*"[16]

The system capabilities[17] are the unyielding indicators to sustain political and economic systems on a solid footing. If these system capabilities work efficiently, political and economic systems will be sustained longer. That consequently supports the cultural and social domains.

In the twenty-first century, India is striving hard to sustain its socio-political and economic systems by opening up its traditional outlook and giving way to foreign goods. After modernization, India also intends to be more tolerant, liberal, and democratic. Its stance on resolving the Kashmir issue is a pertinent example. Indian prospects for democracy are increasing or decreasing, which can be observed objectively through Indian policies in world politics. Those are very akin to that of superpowers based on selective morality.

Contrary to this, Jagdish Bhagwati, who writes *In Defence of Globalization,* believes that globalization has increased the prospects of democracy in the world. For example, he thinks that Indian farmers are no longer exploited by intermediaries owing to the use of computers and the sale of their crops independently.

> "Soybean farmer Mohammad Arif, 24, says the computer allows farmers greater control over their goods. Farmers often get cheated at markets or stuck with the price offered that day. With the computer, he says, they can make a considered decision at home, holding crops until prices improve."[18]

Therefore, it is positive for the Indians to take advantage of the latest technology. It is happening in a domestic framework that is undoubtedly good for India. However, living in an international community, nations must consider that democratic values are also necessary for sustaining themselves respectfully in the community of nations. Hence, we must rely on some universally accepted norms to dig out globalization and its impact on the Indian political system.

In this age of collectivism, every country loves to live according to the contemporary needs and demands of the international community. India also wishes to adopt new ways to live itself lively in modern-day politics through the politics of giving and taking. Therefore, it resolves border disputes with China and other geographically contiguous countries.

One of the major precipitating factors behind India's shift towards an open economy in the 1990s was the collapse of the Soviet Union. On account of the drop in the trade volumes with the Soviet Union and increased oil prices during the Persian Gulf War, Indian Prime Minister P V. Narasimha Rao decided to welcome foreign investment that boosted the Indian economy.[19] After the end of the Cold War in 1991, India started thinking pragmatically to review its political options and decided to open it up for international assistance. It wished to play an essential role in world politics and detonated its nuclear explosions in May 1998. Since then, it has demanded a permanent member status in the Security Council of the U.N. For this, India has to prove itself as a peace-loving nation by resolving its border disputes with all its neighboring countries. By resolving only the Kashmir dispute with Pakistan, India could show itself as a progressive, liberal, peace-loving, democratic, and secular country among the community of nations as it is a prerequisite for permanent membership in the Security Council. Therefore, it can be derived that the last decade of the twentieth century was a reform era in world politics owing to the reunification of East and West Germany in 1990 and the disintegration of the Soviet Union in 1991.

These incidents force certain countries to review their political setups; if a superpower could disintegrate, why would any other developing country become dysfunctional due to its outdated socio-political and economic systems? That admonishes two regional powers, China and India, and one crucial South Asian player, Pakistan, to re-look into their political systems and update them according to the world's increased interconnectedness.

In 1962, the China-India War created border disputes between China and India. China and India resolved their border dispute in Sikkim when Prime Minister Wen Jiabao visited India in April 2004.[20] Arunachal Pradesh is another hot spot where both countries are still hanging in the balance for settling their differences. Since 2003, China and India have appointed special representatives to resolve this border issue as early as possible. Friday, 20 July 2007, was the 10th round of talks between China and India.[21] "China has solved border disputes with ten neighbors except for India and Bhutan," said Indian Defense Minister Pranab Mukherjee.[22]

Nevertheless, India never thinks about why it is unwilling to resolve its border disputes with Pakistan. That can be equally good for India's peaceful environment in the region. These are hegemonic tendencies, deep-rooted in regional powers they can hardly get rid of. China always looks down upon India, and India does it towards Pakistan. If India is interested in leading the region, it has to be rational, democratic, and tolerant. Irrational, undemocratic, and intolerant can never attain Indian leadership in the region. Here is a three-prone formula to become a leader of the region for India.

First, it has to be wise in handling its people and giving them a place in the political system. All substate actors can be amalgamated into the system with unconditional tolerance, as America and Britain have successfully done. The caste system can be uprooted to attain this objective. All states in India can be given equal sharing in economic fruits to keep the 'distributive capability' of the system alive. The latter part of this chapter will discuss how Indian states are selectively dealt with in sharing the economic fruits of the country, which is a natural source of dissatisfaction among the masses.

Second, it has to be secular pragmatically, not vocally. Actions speak louder than words. All religions in India can have an equal say in the country to make it progress, prosperous, and peaceful.

Third, it must resolve all border and other disputes with neighboring countries to ensure a peaceful environment. Then, it can look towards the international system for a respectable global player status.

By using computers, cyberspace, and multimedia, no nation can become progressive and peaceful; it is only democratic ideals, norms, and values that make any country sustainable. Democracy is a complex form of government as it demands too much from the people, for example, their vigilance towards their duties, tolerance for other communities, patience for listening to others, and morality to hold all together.

The essence of democracy does not lie in controlling the minds of people by alluring them through different means of advertisement or marketing. Democracy gives an individual a free hand to think over anything he wants and make a free judgment with his thoughts without any pressure. The industrialized world is interested in hurried pursuits of free markets without considering the consequences that may jeopardize democracy in the newly independent nations.

Realizing the authenticity of democratic ideals for the development of any political system is a hard nut to crack. China has an authoritarian system that bounces back the commercial and free-market forces without consideration and has emerged as an economic giant in Southeast Asia. Acculturation is not the solution to the problem. The countries that import democracy and multiparty parliamentary systems usually lack the capabilities and resources to build a civil society that allows democratic political institutions to work effectively.[23] "Without Civil Society, there can be no citizens, and thus no meaningful democracy."[24] It means democracy needs homework.

Democracy is a gradual process that flourishes with time. Traditional democracies like Britain, Switzerland, and America had to sacrifice a lot to gain democratic ideals, and hundreds of years were taken to have democracy. Even then, flames of discontent existed in such societies.[25] A magical wand cannot install democracy overnight.

It is believed that new technology or scientific advancement plays a vital role in the socio-political and economic development of the country. Besides numerous other sectors, technology provides efficient medical services through medical devices, diagnoses, and treatments. Likewise, the Chinese Chunyu Yisheng app, India's Health Cube, offers a range of medical facilities such as online diagnosis, online medical records, and prescriptions by medical experts.[26] Through this communication age, India has to learn how to dissolve its horizontal and vertical cleavages instantly, which had been resolved by the West more than a hundred years after its birth. Therefore, this age of globalization can be advantageous for 'transitional societies' to learn a lesson from 'traditional societies' and go ahead without further delay.

Western MNCs and diasporas have a significant role in developing India's informatics sector. The influence of the Indian diaspora on informatics is no different than that of the overseas Chinese. Likewise, Chinese immigrants and Indian diasporas acted as conduits of technology and resources into their homeland.[27] Unfortunately, the latest technology and scientific advancement are being used for disparaging goals about hegemony in the region and capturing more world economic resources through immoral means like degradation of the environment and social values (details will come later in this chapter).

In this age of increased interconnectedness, India has accepted that Kashmir is a disputed territory in the region. However, it was not ready to consider a disputed area ever before. It looks pretty positive in resolving the Kashmir issue with Pakistan, and Pakistan is ready to follow suit to sustain good relations with India.

It was one side of the coin. Now, take another look at different dissatisfied segments of Indian society. They always clamor for their helplessness living in India. It is ungratified for Indian democracy to ensure its credibility in the globalized world. It may be Christians, Hindus, Muslims, and Sikhs who are making complaints about the Indian government's subjectivity towards them. Subjectivity is ubiquitous worldwide, even in societies considered democratic to a certain extent. It is the media that exaggerates anything among the masses. Undoubtedly, Western media is more robust than Indian media. Therefore, India usually imitates what the West is holding for its interests. Western media rarely publicizes the dictatorship of the American president or the British cabinet. It always propagates against the developing world's anomalies.

According to former finance secretary Bimal Jalan, 1990-91 was "among the cruelest in India's post-independence economic history".[28] Dr. Manmohan Singh can be considered Gorbachev for India. He is willing to resolve all backlogs for sustainable political and economic development in India. He has been the financing minister of India since the 1990s; therefore, he knows the value of a sustainable economy. He may be feeling pressure from fanatic Hindus to normalize relations with his neighbors.

"I am convinced that the 21st Century will be an Indian Century. The world will again look at us with regard and respect, not just for the economic progress we make but for the democratic values we cherish and uphold and the principles of pluralism and inclusiveness we have come to represent, which is India's heritage."[29] India has to be more pragmatic in its actions, which always speak louder than words. Now, we proceed towards India's political placement in the future.

India's Political Placement in the Future

Interestingly, India's future political placement is conditioned on these major elements: how successfully has it saved its social system? Second, how does it save its environment in the process of industrialization? (Details regarding environmental degradation in India will come later in this chapter). Third, how does it resolve the crises of governance? Fourth, how does it face the challenges of globalization through regionalism? Regionalism is a countercurrent of globalization.

Regional integration is considered an alternative to globalization. That can be sustained in the community of nations in the twenty-first century. Kenichi

Ohmae writes in his *The End of the Nation-State: The Rise of Regional Economies* that everything in this century is reshaping. Capital, corporations, consumers, and communication are the primary determinants that are underpinning the phenomenon of regionalism to dominate over the world. European Union is a success story in this regard, but in the third world or the developing world, ASEAN, G7, G8, G20, G77, SAARC, Shanghai 5, and Shanghai Cooperation Organization all are classic examples of rising regionalism with a wild goose chase. Regionalism may prove a direct result of globalization.

Globalization has compressed the world and space through the communication revolution that also assisted the process of regionalism. The nation-state may not be sustained without this regional integration. It will also earn peace and friendship in the world instead of violence, hatred, and animosity if it is based on morality rather than selective morality. Therefore, it can be derived that pragmatic regionalism dominated with 'isothymia' part of the soul in which parity among nations is a prerequisite.

Sunil rightly suggested that India has to act as an international player who could bridge the relations between two big powers, China and the U.S., as a 'bridging power.' Although such a role is not found in the political world, India can make it an experiment. It should not only become a bridge between big and small powers but can also work as a moderator between the rich and the poor or even between rival developing countries. But before taking such a role, India must redefine its political character in its neighborhood. Without good relations with neighboring countries, ensuring the international community that India can work as a 'bridging power is challenging, as Sunil suggested.

Indian policymakers must be vigilant in using their skills in the modern world and act accordingly. They must know how to use and "when to use its economic resources, 'coercive diplomacy,' moral legitimacy, or capacity for dialogue, to serve its interests."

It is said that the U.S. may use India as a buffer state against China. But India has to be a good friend of China for playing an essential role in world politics. As mentioned earlier, good relations with neighbors are essential for international exposure on sound grounds. America is just using Asian countries for the time being. It intends to control and monopolize lucrative economic markets in India and China and urges to have control of the oil politics of the region. Therefore, to fulfill its objectives successfully, the U.S. is legitimately using its strategic tactics. It is now up to the Asian countries how they manage to escape that American influence with their survival. They cannot deny the preponderance of the U.S. in the modern world. Hence, they must balance good relations with good friends and a fair-weather friend.

India's latest civil nuclear deal in 2007 categorically exposes its hegemonic designs. In the pretext of this deal, India is losing its autonomy in world affairs as America may dictate its terms upon India. The U.S. is pressurizing India for not embarking on the India-Pakistan Iran energy pipeline project. This project is absolutely in the Indian national interest along with its members. Hence, the U.S. is unhappy with this project owing to its advantages with three member countries. Therefore, India has to withdraw itself from this project later or sooner.

India is a regional power and shares a respectable status in the community of nations. Asia has to be very watchful about its political goals as regional integration may give rise to 'glocalization' (think locally and act globally). It will benefit India if it gives importance to neighboring countries, especially China and Pakistan. China, India, Iran, Pakistan, and Russia can work together to sustain a prosperous future of Asia by dissolving all regional organizations (SAARC, ECO, and ASEAN) and amalgamating them into one unit, which may be the Asian Union. Asian Union can benefit the member countries' political, economic, and social conditions.

India's Economic Interests

India is an emerging economy in the world. It is very much based on a capitalist cum socialist economy. It has been flourishing differently in the twenty-first century. It claims to be a market-free economy. However, it has been a mixed economy. Indian economic reforms started in the 1980s. The Indian economy was never opened as much as it is today. In this part of the chapter, we explore that India is making considerable headway in its economy based on sustainable economic development. It may be a big claim as different parts of India are unsatisfied with the ongoing economic development in India. We should try to explore globalization and its impact on the Indian economy in three domains:

Indian Economy in the Past

Mahatma Gandhi was a chief exponent of self-governance in India and opposed state control over the economic life of the people.[30] India had been very confident about its historical legacy of economic nationalism and considered its consumer products the best in the world. It has been beautiful for the world's economic market.[31] After the War of Plassey in 1757 and the War of Independence in 1857, the Indian economy was swayed by British control through a transnational corporation named the East India Company. The Britishers gradually uprooted Indian industry and agriculture and undermined the very nature of its economic system, which was based on self-governance.

For a historical analysis of the Indian economy for the last fifty years, we must rely upon Bradford de Long and Gurcharan Das[32]. They said:

> "….between 1900 and 1950 (under the British Raj), India's real GDP grew 0.7 percent a year (implying a decline in per capita income); between 1950 and 1980, real GDP grew at an average pace of 3.7 percent per year (and per capita income just 1.5percent), marginally above the global average for that period; but then real GDP accelerated to 5.9 percent growth (and per capita income to 3.8 percent) in the 1980-90 period, and to 6.2 percent(with per capita income growing 4.4 percent) annually in the 1990-8."[33]

The next part of this chapter is mainly based on the views furnished by Prasenjit K. Basu, Managing Director of Robust Economic Analysis (Pvt.) Ltd. It is an economic research and consultancy company based in Singapore. He also writes a fortnightly column for The Edge (a financial weekly published in Singapore and Malaysia). He has shared his views in the International Herald Tribune, The Statesman (India), and Economic Bulletin.[34]

Asia accounts for the world's 30 percent of billionaires, and India ranks at the top comparatively, except the United States, China, and Russia. Family businesses serve as the backbone of Asian economies. Out of the world's 500 largest family businesses, one-fifth are located in East Asia, with China and India constituting the most significant number; 85 percent of India's companies are backed by family businesses that comprise two-thirds of its GDP.[35] For the last twenty or more years, India's GDP has grown at an average of 5.9 percent per year. It is a tremendous development with such a large population, and sustaining it for two decades is not a joke. Mr. Basu says, "India's economic achievement is unprecedented and should therefore have qualified to be labeled an 'economic miracle.' Most commentators appear unaware that India has grown faster than all the Asian "miracle" economies (save China) since 1992."[36] He named India as the "stealth miracle economy."

In the 1950s, Nehru was more focused on import-substituting industrialization (ISI) as recommended by the WB for economic development in India. Mr. Basu said:

> "The ISI strategy was also founded on the belief (among developed economies) that the developing countries would primarily substitute imports of consumer goods with domestic production but would still need to import capital goods (and probably most intermediates) from the developed world. It was argued that the successful growth of the developing countries would boost their demand for capital goods – so the ISI strategy was seen as a win-win situation for both sides."

The main factor that made the ISI unsuccessful in India was that it protected the domestic industry with high tariffs and non-tariff barriers. This created an unfavorable balance of trade in India, and the then-export products (agricultural commodities, minerals, and textiles) suffered greatly due to the unfavorable trade balance.

Despite the unfavorable balance of trade and the resulting balance of payments crisis in 1957-58, India contentedly attained a GDP growth of 4 percent per year, somewhat better than the international community of that time. On the other hand, the wars with China in 1962 and Pakistan in 1965 took a heavy toll on the meager Indian economy.

The second Prime Minister of India, Lal Bahadur Shastri, took the first step toward the Green Revolution with the concentration of powers in the office of the Prime Minister. In January 1966, Indira Gandhi, India's third Prime Minister, adopted market-based policies until 1969. At the outset, a 57 percent depreciation of the rupee and lethargy in the adoption of export incentives faced a rebellion from the old guard of the Congress party, replaced her with the Deputy Prime Minister and finance minister, Morarji Desai, who guided very well India's during the 1957 balance of payments crisis. Later on, Indira Gandhi came into power in the late 1960s and early 1970s, leading India to domestic and external uncertainties. She took a substantial loan of U.S.$5 billion from the IMF for Structural Adjustment and gave a guarantee to have a growth rate of 5 percent per year for reducing poverty.[37] Ultimately, she met her account in the early 1980s.

She adopted the policies of economic nationalism and sent them back to Coca-Cola and IBM from India. However, IBM played an essential role in software development in India. That created a vacuum for soft hardware in India for some time but was instantly filled by domestic companies like Tata Consultancy Services or TCS, Wipro, Hindustan Computers Ltd, or HCL. These companies led India's information technology (IT) revolution in the 1990s.

Rajiv Gandhi continued structural reforms from 1984 to 1989 as Prime Minister at a reticent speed; industrial de-licensing made a little more progress, and gradual liberalization of imports continued. He also softened the tax reforms and extracted the resources more efficiently than his mother. He employed the advantage of the IT revolution and encouraged the use of computers in essential government departments and companies. Even facing strong opposition, he made reforms in the telecommunications system.

During the balance of payments crisis in 1991, Prime Minister P.V. Narasimha Rao appointed Dr. Manmohan Singh as finance minister and assigned him the task of sweeping structural economic reforms. The fragile alliance-based governments headed by VP Singh (November 1989-November 1990) and Chandrasekhar (December 1989-May 1991) depleted India's foreign exchange reserves in the wake of the first Gulf War in 1991.

After the assassination of Rajiv Gandhi in 1991, the Indian political system faced political instability until the late nineties. That established a "sympathy wave" in favor of Congress for the time being, but it could not earn as much advantage.

Even during political instability, foreign reserves have continued to proliferate. U.S.$ 127 billion at the end of November 2004 provided more than 17 months' import cover. On the other hand, exports also responded well. In the late nineties, when East Asian currencies depreciated, the Indian rupee sustained owing to the export boom in India. Mr. Basu writes:

> "Services exports have done even better, growing even when the rupee was appreciating against the dollar —even though nearly two-thirds of all software exports go to the U.S. market. Software exports decelerated slightly in the aftermath of the bursting of the 1999-2000 bubble in the IT- "dot-com" sector... exports of "Invisibles" (services, transfers, and investment income) have risen nearly seven-fold, fromU.S.$7.49 billion in the twelve months to June 1991 to U.S.$59.1 billion in the 12 months to June 2004."

India had been a country where economic nationalism was very much in vogue after independence. Therefore, India could recognize itself as an independent state, experiencing 'autarky' (economic self-sufficiency). Historically, India has been mesmerized by its bureaucracy since Jawaharlal Lal Nehru. He can be considered the first culprit for making the Indian economy meager at the outset. The Indian bureaucrats planned that India would not have imports under Nehru's policy of economic self-sufficiency. India could not produce quality goods due to a lack of resources and an inflated population. India failed to win laurels in its economic development with the Nehruvian approach based on the Soviet Union-styled central planning.[38] Although Mr. C. Raj Gopal Acharya, Minoo Massani, and Nijjalingappa did their best to bring home the Indian bureaucracy, reforms in the name of equity are inefficient and destroy the Indian economy.[39] In the 1970s, a rural movement was started by thousands of farmers of India in Andhra, Gujrat, Haryana, Maharashtra, and Punjab to have free trade in domestic as well as international markets.[40]

After the assassination of Indira Gandhi in 1984, Rajiv Gandhi was the first ruler in India who ended the bureaucratic influence of economic planning by saying: "A poor country cannot afford to carry on billing the poorest people for its inefficiency and call itself socialist."[41] Rajiv Gandhi was frustrated with India's technological backwardness and played a significant role in developing India's IT industry. He wanted to introduce modern technology; in 1984, he became ready to implement policies to modernize Indian technology through private companies and welcoming Western companies.[42]

The regional economies of India were sinking very severely. For example, the core states in India, comprising Madhya Pradesh, Rajasthan, and Maharashtra, have more land, but the states in the periphery, like eastern Indian Uttar Pradesh and Bihar, have more population owing to their meager literacy and highest birth and mortality rates.[43] This imbalance kept Indian regional economies at the lowest ebb. It has always been there that countries usually take more care of their core states as compared to the peripheral states. In the last chapter, we saw that it was also happening in China. Manipur, Bihar, Orissa, Tripura, and Uttar Pradesh remained underprivileged until 1991. We can see Madhya Pradesh did considerable development by 1991 due to the economic reforms of Rajiv Gandhi. It is not necessary that regional states can only be developed through government policies. In Kerala's case, we can credit civil society for eliminating poverty from that state until the end of the twentieth century. All that development was focused on health and education, less on growth.[44]

Therefore, commitment on the part of individuals to be a participant is the sine qua non for eternal and visible development in any domain. We see that Nehru's policy of economic self-sufficiency encouraged domestic economic growth and gave rise to protectionism (an economic process in which local business is protected against foreign goods through curtailing imports in the country) in India remained unsuccessful. Rajiv Gandhi's reforms kept India on the road to economic prosperity. It was an international environment that disallowed India to keep itself aloof from economic progress with one of the largest lucrative economic markets in the world. Therefore, in this age of globalization, India couldn't detach itself from the world economy by adopting the Nehruvian approach.

In the last two decades of the twentieth century, India started opening up its economy and giving way to certain imported goods. Diaspora professionals at American MNCs contributed to outsourcing massive services from the U.S. to India. Therefore, migration does not only lead to brain drain instead, but it can also serve as a source of "brain" as well as capital gain if advanced nations provide conducive domestic conditions.[45] Domestic constraints kept India busy resolving its horizontal and vertical cleavages regarding linguistic, parochial, or biased and everlasting lacuna between haves and have-nots. With the communication revolution, India has to cope with the situation and decided to go for outsourcing, which is an integral part of increased interconnectedness.

Indian Economy at Present

Urbanization has increased pressure on urban areas in India. It also has augmented the gap between the rural and urban elite. That gap has created a vacuum in the Indian economic system and inflated poverty in rural India. The Indian government is feeling that pressure and has decided to face it prudently. Again, development is happening in India in core states, and the population is increasing in the peripheral states. This is a significant threat to India at the domestic level. It can only be resolved through the cooperation of the masses and efficient and people-oriented policies by the government.

Owing to the tremendous population size and fewer resources in the country, skilled and nonskilled social capital in India used to go overseas for opportunities to earn more and more for the prosperity of their family. It detaches the individual from participating in the system. This aloofness from the system directly affects the economic system, owing to a loss in skilled and nonskilled social capital at home. Therefore, this brain drain process is negatively undermining the country. On the other hand, overseas earnings sent back to India are part of the Indian economy and are used to sustain its economic infrastructure.

During the macroeconomic crises in the early 1990s, India adopted economic liberalism under the leadership of P.V. Narasimha Rao. In the late 1990s, the Indian economy was $1,702.7 trillion, which was almost 5% of world income. In the first five years of the twenty-first century, the Indian economy rose to $3,815.6 trillion, worth 6.3% of world income. It was considered the fourth largest in the world as far as GDP was concerned.[46]

India, the Philippines, and Thailand focus on privatizing airlines, dairies, casinos, and nearly everything to stimulate commercial activities. To ensure better corporate governance, the Indian government is constrained to relax foreign investment regulations. Moreover, privatization is accelerated to eliminate high financial and non-financial corporate debt levels.[47]

India is not utilizing its economic infrastructure more efficiently as it is not enjoying good political relations with its neighbors. Without good political relations, hardly any country can earn laurels in the international political economy. Owing to mobilizing its forces on borders, especially on Siachin, that is the highest point of the war in the world where the cost of war is so immense and undermining the economies of both India and Pakistan. If India prudently resolves its border relations with Pakistan, as it did recently with China, it will go beyond expectations in its economic development. However, it will also benefit Pakistan's economy and ultimately help India play a positive and peaceful role in world politics. Therefore, peaceful and prosperous neighbors would assist India in the community of nations.

India has immense talent and resources; it has to use such capabilities effectively to maximize its international position; it has to understand the real meaning of power that relates to relative meanings and can be understood from different perspectives in different circumstances. Military, arms, and technology are also used as power, but in the twenty-first century, using capabilities and skills at the proper time for a proper case can earn a lot and boost the economy of any country to a level of satisfaction. For instance, China does not interfere in world affairs or allow them to poke their nose into their affairs. China is using the capabilities and skills of its social capital according to the circumstances without considering how the world looks at its manufacturing standard. It is producing consumer goods for every individual in the world.

Therefore, India has to take a leaf out of the Chinese book for economic development based on good relations with its neighbors and manufacturing consumer goods for the entire world with the policy of non-aggrandizement. We have a history that arms and armies never win the people's hearts, but peace and love can. India has to be realistic in this perspective and have to liberate Kashmir with dignity and concentrate on developing its boosting economy. If India keeps aggravating its neighbors' conflicts, it will not sustain its ongoing surging economic prosperity.

It has been stated in the theoretical framework of our research that system capabilities play an essential role in developing a political system. Hence, it is not only good GDP and growth rates that give a state recognition in the community of nations, but the state also can extract its resources (collecting taxes, etc.) and its ability to regulate them efficiently.

Indian Economy in the Future

In the future, the Indian economy can increase its growth rate only if it is based on the equitable distribution of wealth through the trickle-down effect. As mentioned in the previous discussion, most Indian states remained deprived of certain economic fruits that increased poverty in such regional peripheral states. India has to increase the credibility of its institutions among the masses. It is only possible when the Indian economic infrastructure will plan for the whole Indian community based on parity. The ongoing increasing lacuna between haves and have-nots is due to India's dynastic politics.

The actual economic figures give us an optimistic view of the Indian political system. The present government is protecting the national interest and making steady improvements in the economic domain. It seems that India's real GDP will increase in the future. Manjeet Kripalani and Pete Engardio write in the Rise of India:

> "India produces about 3.1 million college graduates each year11, 50 percent more than the 2 million churned out by the next biggest producer of graduates (the U.S.). Of these, about 260,000 are engineering and science graduates—again, a considerable lead over the U.S. and everybody else. Tertiary enrolment — especially in engineering, technical, and management schools — is rising rapidly and is expected to rise 50 percent from last year's levels by 2008."[48]

The ongoing pace of Indian political and economic development shows that Calcutta, Delhi, Bangalore, and Hyderabad, with original software and IT services, are experiencing rapid growth. Several other cities and towns will develop soon, like Ahmedabad, Bhubaneswar, Chennai, Guwahati, Jalandhar, Kanpur, Lucknow, and Pune. This development shows that India will continue its leadership in software after Israel in the future and may overcome Israel's software exports in the next two decades. Mr. Basu also shared the same view and wrote:

> "While software export revenues are just 2.5 percent of GDP now, they should rise to 6 to 7 percent of GDP by 2008 – and total "invisible" exports should rise from the current 13 percent to nearer 25 percent of GDP by 2010."

It seems that India may grow at 7 percent per year for the next decade, owing to its knowledge-based industry and textiles. The development of biotechnology will also profoundly impact the agriculture sector. Suppose bureaucratic red tape remains detached from the ongoing economic development in India. In that case, we can expect the fiscal situation to improve, and real GDP growth will increase to 8 to 8.5 percent per year in the decade ahead.

Look at the following graph, which predicts that India may be the third-largest economy by 2035.

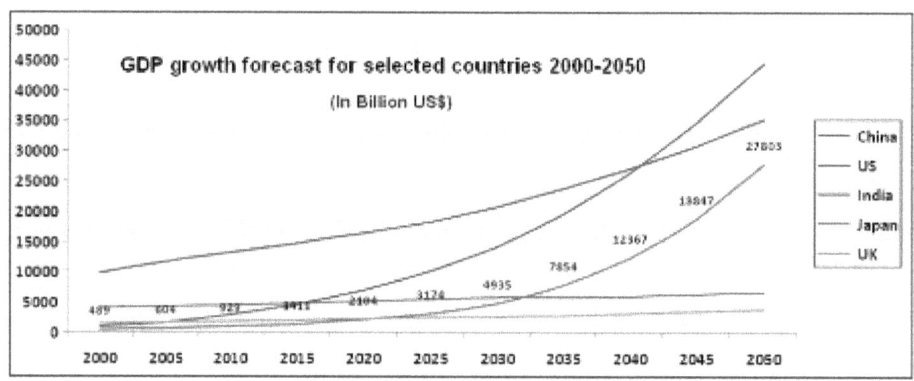

Goldman Sachs has predicted that India will become the third-largest economy in the world by 2035, based on a growth rate of 5.3 to 6.1%. Currently, it is cruising at a 9.2% growth rate.
Source: http://en.wikipedia.org/wiki/Economy_of_India. The website was visited on 20-05-07.

All these facts cannot be considered credible until an ordinary man in India is not getting the fruits of globalization. Literature review shows that in India, most people are unsatisfied with the ongoing reforms as they do not give any credit to the people. There is no trickle-down effect usually claimed by the public sector in India. A typical Indian can perceive his economic freedom only in the uniform implementation of reforms in India. For example, the following steps can enhance people's trust in its political and economic systems:[49]

- Removing corruption and kickbacks from the public and private sectors encourages people to interact more actively with the system.
- Decentralization to the grassroots level could empower people, not government officials, to start private businesses, boosting the Indian economy at the micro and macro levels.
- People must feel security in sustaining their private assets for a prosperous life.
- Speedy justice should be provided to people to satisfy them mentally and physically for not being deprived of their fundamental rights.

Socio-Cultural Effects

"How can a society make economic and cultural progress which devalues its inherited legacy of skills and declares more than 90 percent of its people as 'backward,' 'most backward' and 'scheduled castes' and declares them as lacking intelligence and capability, simply because their knowledge is not acquired through the formal education system and textbooks written in the English language."[50]

Indian culture is the only domain that seems affected by globalization. It is affected negatively to an extent as we see Indian Bollywood does not represent authentic Indian culture. Indian media, especially television in India, produces programs that hardly depict the social phenomenon happening in India. We believe that Indian media is tormenting the Indian glorious heritage in this age of globalization. This is a big difference between China and India as earlier follows the West keeping its values intact, while the latter seems guilty in this domain.

Parag Khanna manages the Global Governance Initiative of the World Economic Forum, based at the Brookings Institution in Washington, D.C., and explains how globalization deeply affects Indian culture.

He called Indian commercial developments on a large scale "Bollystan, a realm in which Indian roots are planted everywhere, but the flowering of the trees traces back only loosely to the original seed."[51]

He further says Bollystan is rising physically as a "bowl of Ethno-commerce and a new model of geographically transcendent sovereignty." India produces movies, microchips, and Miss Universes on a large scale but cannot regulate them even if such ventures are being produced beyond Indian borders. The era of globalization is affecting the Indian social system with 'migration of dreams' and 'relative deprivations.

Western apparel brands aim to grab the attention of Indian urban elites. Still, the paramount status of well-known Indian designers like Manish Malhotra, Tarun Tahiliani, and Ritu Kumar will make West Indianize compete. Besides the fashion industry, the Indian film industry has been no stranger to global outreach. In the 1950s, as an antidote to Hollywood poison, the USSR was obsessed with Indian films. In the 1980s, Bollywood gained fame to the extent that the Egyptian government had to limit Indian film screening because of the threat to local film revenues.[52]

Indians are so busy singing, dancing, and producing music that it has become difficult for an intellectual to be recognized owing to its literary piece. Indian remix songs and cross-border cinematographics have made India so commercial that it may make India global in such domains but will lose certain intellectuals amidst deprivation and alienation. Parag Khanna says, "Culture, not politics, lies at the heart of Bollystan."

At the 2004 Edinburgh International Book Festival invited Indian authors like Anita Desai, Hari Kunzru, and newcomer Siddharth Shangvi, there were very few who showed their reverence towards them. Undoubtedly, Amitabh Bachchan stood at the top in the BBC's online poll to name an "actor of the Millennium." In the New York Times, Prashant Agarwal argues, "The day will come when Bollywood stars are just as famous in the United States as they are in India."[53]

Once Joel Kotkin said, "Do not surrender their sense of a particular ethnic identity at the altar of technology or science but utilize their historically conditioned values and beliefs to cope successfully with change."[54]

In the contemporary era, Indians have produced an interconnected civilization, as did the Anglo-Saxons, Chinese, and Jews.

India's vast population is spread all over the world. The modern world shares the Indian population with a significant number. In almost forty-eight countries, Indians number at least ten thousand. In other countries, it ranges from one lac to half a million.

The Middle East, the U.K., the U.S., and other European countries comprise a larger community with a good say in those systems. After India, China again has a larger dispersed population size worldwide. In the U.S., which has almost six million nationals overseas, neither democrats nor republicans give importance to immigrants, such as the extension of Social Security benefits and other issues regarding citizenship and nationality of the newly born babies.

Asia now entices American millennials, and 80 percent believe that Asia is the perfect destiny for being the most critical region, guaranteeing a better future.[55] The preponderance of Indian Americans is increasing in the U.S. compared to the U.K. Indian Americans are a very wealthy ethnic group in the U.S. with an estimated income of $60,093 that, is double as compared to the local Americans and boasting 200,000 millionaires.[56]

Indians have membership in essential institutions related to technology and financial affairs. Many professional and social organizations exist, from the American Association of Physicians of Indian Origin to the Indian National Overseas Congress. Despite all these organizations, earning a lot of money is an essential first step for gaining influence in the democratic marketplace. Parag Khana writes, "A half-century after Dilip Singh Saund became the first Indian American to serve in Congress, Republican whiz kid Bobby Jindal won a seat in the House of Representatives from Louisiana in the recent U.S. election."

Few groups in America, like the U.S.-India Political Action Committee (USINPAC), are playing an essential role in determining the political future of key U.S. political figures. This group chose the New York Senator Hillary Clinton for the Senate's growing "Friends of India" committee. In 2002, the same USINPAC caused a defeat to Cynthia McKinney, a five-term Congresswoman from Georgia, who was pro-Pakistan and Khalistan. Although she got another seat from Georgia, and now Jindal had joined back in the House.

Parag Khana further explains that scores of Indians had formal roles in the 2004 Republican and Democratic national conventions and had raised millions on both sides of the American political scene. Both presidential candidates submitted and appreciated the vitality of the Indian American community in the U.S. and promised to appoint them at the level of cabinet and sub-cabinet positions. The Indian community has become so important in America that it has become an obligation for the American president to visit India before he elected to have the attention of the Indian American community in the U.S., such a visit would be like visiting one of the European capitals.

Many Indian students study in America every year and adopt American values. Almost 80,000 Indian students in the U.S., the most from any country, are learning about technical education. The Bush government is very anxious about having bilateral relations with India, more than "Next Steps for Strategic Partnership." The result is that the Indian American community consistently pressurized the U.S. government and lobbied for a permanent Indian seat in the United Nations Security Council.

India is guilty in the domains of human rights violations, democratic ideals, the rule of law, and gender discrimination that is worst in the form of wedding rituals based on dowry at the time of marriage and the custom of 'Satti' (setting ablaze to a widow with the death of her husband). The unbiased analysis shows that degradation in the social system hardly undermines a political system. Still, environmental degradation not only undermines a political system through diseases among human beings but also affects the economic system on a large scale.

> "The increase in sexual violence, wife murders, escalating dowries, corruption, female feticide, declining sex ratio, increasing crime in our society, the impoverished condition and indebtedness of our farmers, failure of crops due to poor quality pesticides, the growing frustrations of millions of unemployed youths in India-all these and more are projected as inevitable outcomes of the process of globalization...."[57]

Globalization and Environmental Degradation in India

Globalization is a natural process in which development takes place in all domains of life and usually takes a heavy toll on the environment. India is developing by leaps and bounds and installing industry to fulfill the needs and demands of the people in time without protecting the environmental concerns.

This ongoing rapid progress may take India to the level of the third-largest economy in the world. Still, the future of the next generation will be murky owing to the depletion of the ozone layer and the greenhouse effect. It is happening due to consistent carbon dioxide emissions in the environment in the wake of industrialization in India. Calcutta ranks at the top for being India's most polluted city. Pollution leads to more than 2.5 million deaths each year.[58]

It is a debate in India that there are environmental consequences India faces for economic development. It swept water, forests, and air under its sway on a large scale. Water scarcity has always been ordinary in India's urban and rural areas.[59] In rural areas, water is usually under the control of upper-caste Hindus, and they do not allow the lower-caste Hindus to use that water according to their needs.[60] The quantity of water is not the only problem; the quality is more dangerous for people's health.

"The urban elites fit expensive filtration and purification units to their kitchenware supply, and many drink bottled water. Many urban and rural people are exposed to water rich in herbicides, pesticides, industrial chemicals, and sewage."[61] The condition of the industrial sector is worse than this. Many industries in India are disposing of their raw wastes in the rivers. The leather tanneries are also disposing of their waste chemicals into the water. The cloth dyeing industries are other culprits for destroying the Indian water reservoirs.[62] Laws are made for protecting the environment but not abiding by the people. Red tape and kickback culture among government officials are ruining the environment in India more rapidly.[63]

Most of the world's largest coal-producing companies are in China, while South Asia has the world's most filthy cities like Karachi, Mumbai, Delhi, and

Dhaka[64] Dumping is another aspect that is polluting the environment in India. It is happening in India that it imports waste from rich states and recycles it for usage. In India, it was supported that many products can be made by recycling imported waste, which means the availability of cheaper goods. In the Basle Convention 1989, dumping was prohibited in India, but recycling was permitted. According to Praful Bidwai, "It is either disingenuous or unethical to argue that waste imports are good because they generate employment, without considering the quality of that employment and its consequences for the employee as well as the larger environment, air, flora and fauna and, above all, people. Beyond a point, jobs at any cost is a perverse argument."[65] It is expected that when natural resources fulfill the needs of everyday life, it threatens the environment. People even like trees for shadows and fruits, but they also need wood for making furniture, plows, tools, and paper, and the leaves of trees are also used as utensils and other things for their daily use. Indian NGOs did their best to bring people home and teach them about harvesting trees without cutting them down. The main biomass demands in India are fuel and fodder. The need for fuel is usually fulfilled through vegetable resources in both rural and towns.[66]

The Indian government is trying to make dams to end water scarcity in the country and disseminate information about the usefulness of natural habitats among the masses. Now, we compare two countries and how they are affected by globalization in the twenty-first century.

Endnotes

1 http://www.wordwebonline.com/search.pl?ww=3&w=consociational. Website visited on 13-12-06.

2 Fareed Zakaria, *The Future of Freedom: Illiberal Democracy Home and Abroad,* New York: W.W. Norton & Company, 2004, 106.

3 Parag Khanna, *THE FUTURE IS ASIAN: Commerce, Conflict, and Culture in the 21st Century*: Simon & Schuster, 2019, 275-276.

4 M.J. Akbar, "The Moral Code of Indian Democracy," *The Dawn,* August 19, 2005.

5 Zakria, *The Future of Freedom,* 107.

6 Ibid.

7 Ibid., 108.

8Ibid.

9 Min Ye, *Diasporas and Foreign Direct Investment in China and India*: Cambridge University Press, 2014, 07.

10 Kishwar, *Deepening democracy,* 5.

11 Sunil Khilnani, India as a Bridging Power, published in 2005 by The Foreign Policy Centre, 49 Chalton Street London.

12 Parag Khanna, *THE FUTURE IS ASIAN: Commerce, Conflict, and Culture in the 21st Century*: Simon & Schuster, 2019, 190-191.

13 Min Ye, *The Belt Road and Beyond: State-Mobilized Globalization in China: 1998-2018*: Cambridge University Press, 2020,115.

14 Parag Khanna, *THE FUTURE IS ASIAN: Commerce, Conflict, and Culture in the 21st Century*: Simon & Schuster, 2019, 135.

15 Min Ye, *Diasporas and Foreign Direct Investment in China and India*: Cambridge University Press, 2014, 183.

16 Kishwar, *Deepening democracy,* 7

17 For details about system capabilities, see the introduction and the first chapter.

18 "Companies Market to India's Have-Littles," *Wall Street Journal,* Thursday, June 5, 2003, B1, B12, cited in Jagdish Bhagwati, *In defence of Globalization,* New York: Oxford University Press, 2004, 93.

19 Parag Khanna, *THE FUTURE IS ASIAN: Commerce, Conflict, and Culture in the 21st Century*: Simon & Schuster, 2019, 61.

20 http://news.indiainfo.com/2005/09/04/0409china-pranab-arunachal.html. Website visited on 17-12-06.

21 *Dawn,* Lahore, Saturday, April 21, 2007, 14.

22 http://news.indiainfo.com/2005/09/04/0409china-pranab-arunachal.html. Ibid.

23 Barber, *Jihad Vs. McWorld,* 234.

24   Ibid.

25 Ibid., 278-79.

26 Parag Khanna, *THE FUTURE IS ASIAN: Commerce, Conflict, and Culture in the 21st Century*: Simon & Schuster, 2019, 187-188.

27 Min Ye, *Diasporas and Foreign Direct Investment in China and India*: Cambridge University Press, 2014, 178.

28 Min Ye, *Diasporas and Foreign Direct Investment in China and India*: Cambridge University Press, 2014, 122

29 Dr. Manmohan Singh, India's Prime Minister, addresses the Indian diaspora at the Pravasi Bhartiya Divas, Mumbai, January 7, 2005.

30 Kishwar, *Deepening Democracy*, 56-57.

31 Ibid., 57.

32 Bradford de Long, India since Independence: An Analytic Growth Narrative (April 2001 draft at http://www.j-bradforddelong. net/Econ_Articles/India/India_Rodrik_draft1.html) and Gurcharan Das, India Unbound, Penguin, New Delhi, 2000. Professor de Long points out that, at the average pace of 1980-2000, India will achieve the per capita income levels of the present-day United States by 2061.

33 Ibid.

34 Prasenjit K. Basu, India, and the Knowledge Economy: The "Stealth Miracle" is Sustainable, published in 2005 by The Foreign Policy Centre 49, Chalton Street London.

35 Parag Khanna, *THE FUTURE IS ASIAN: Commerce, Conflict, and Culture in the 21st Century*: Simon & Schuster, 2019, 149.

36 Ibid.

37 T.N. Srinivasan and Suresh Tendulkar, Reintegrating India with the World Economy, Institute for International Economics, Washington DC, March 2003. Pages 22-23.

38 http://www.sjsu.edu/faculty/watkins/india.htm#REF97. Website visited on 29-06-2007.

39 Kishwar, *Deepening Democracy*, 57.

40 Ibid.

41 http://www.sjsu.edu/faculty/watkins/india.htm. Website visited on 29-06-2007.

42 Min Ye, *Diasporas and Foreign Direct Investment in China and India*: Cambridge University Press, 2014, 180.

43 Ibid.

44 Jagdish Bhagwati, *In Defence of Globalization,* 14.

45 Min Ye, *Diasporas and Foreign Direct Investment in China and India*: Cambridge University Press, 2014, 218.

46 http://en.wikipedia.org/wiki/Timeline_of_the_economy_of_India. Website visited on 29-06-07.

47 Parag Khanna, *The Future is Asian: Commerce, Conflict, and Culture in the 21st Century*: Simon & Schuster, 2019, 158-159.

48 Manjeet Kripalani and Pete Engardio, *The Rise of India*, Business Week, 3 December 2003.

49 Kishwar, *Deepening Democracy*, 56.

50 Ibid., 53.

51 Parag Khana, Bollystan: India's Diasporic Diplomacy, published in 2005 by The Foreign Policy Centre, 49 Chalton Street London.

52 Parag Khanna, *THE FUTURE IS ASIAN: Commerce, Conflict, and Culture in the 21st Century*: Simon & Schuster, 2019, 310-313.

53 "Dream On", *New York Times*, 29 April, 2004.

54 Joel Kotkin, *Tribes*, Random House, 1994.

55 Parag Khanna, *The Future is Asian: Commerce, Conflict, and Culture in the 21st Century*: Simon & Schuster, 2019, 217.

56 Amit Gupta, "The Indian Diaspora's Political Efforts in the United States," ORF Occasional Paper, September 2004.

57 Kishwar, *Deepening Democracy*, 8-9

58 Parag Khanna, *THE FUTURE IS ASIAN: Commerce, Conflict, and Culture in the 21st Century*: Simon & Schuster, 2019, 165.

59 Pamela Shurmer-Smith, *India: Globalization and Change,* London: Oxford University Press Inc., 2000, 148.

60 Ibid.

61 The Environmentalist Journal *Down to Earth*: Analysis: Perpetual Thirst, 1999, 7(19). Cited in Pamela Shurmer-Smith, *India: Globalization and Change,* 149.

62 Ibid.

63 Ibid., 150.

64 Parag Khanna, *The Future is Asian: Commerce, Conflict, and Culture in the 21st Century*: Simon & Schuster, 2019, 165.

65 Praful Bidwai, Toxic Waste Disposal: a ready dumping lot. The Hindu Survey of the Environment, 1996, 191. Cited in Pamela Shurmer-Smith, *India: Globalization and Change,* 152.

66 Ibid., 153.

Chapter 4. Evaluation, Comparison, and Contrast between Chinese and Indian Globalization

In the previous two chapters, we saw the phenomenon of globalization in a theoretical and operational framework in two different political systems: China and India. Here in this chapter, we shall focus on the evaluation, comparison, and contrast between the two countries under discussion. We will evaluate again in three different but significant domains: political, economic, and social.

Here, we also see a few analogies in both political systems: China and India are two populous countries worldwide. Oded Shanker gives a rough estimate of the Chinese population as 1.3 billion compared to the Indian population of nearly 1 billion.[1] Therefore, owing to their populous status worldwide, China and India are at 1 and 2, respectively. They are using their social capital or population in a way that economic development can be seen in China and India. Their skill entire labor is working in the whole world. He thinks that the 'Chinese Diaspora' is occupied with wealth and business while Indians are with education and technological advancement. Both countries are working hard to get out of the dominance of socialism.[2]

Both countries have the oldest civilizations, Confucianism in China and Hinduism in India. They are located in Asia, surrounded by Russia, an immense power. They are in the region with the most significant number of nuclear powers. Those are China, India, Pakistan, and Russia. Therefore, out of seven world nuclear powers, four are found in Asia. That's why a former American president said that Kashmir is a nuclear flashpoint in the world. Both countries are considered big economic giants in the twenty-first century. Now, we compare the two countries, giving us a striking contrast.

Geographically speaking, both China and India are two regional players, along with their global importance. China is a global player and wishes to go together with Asia. Contrary to this, India, as a regional power, wishes for hegemony in the region and being utilized by other powers like the U.S. has been using India consistently after its so-called war against terrorism.

Politically, China and India are entirely different countries. The Communist Party of China rules China, and a semi-democratic federal form of government rules India. India has been a British colony, and China has never been a colony. This is the point where both countries are politically altogether different. The British parliament is considered the mother of all parliaments; therefore, the Indian parliament is a direct outcome of the British Indian Act of 1935. Even with one of the oldest civilizations on the earth, India is still intellectually dependent upon the West for its political layout. After the Partition Act 1947, the first Governor-General of India was a British known as Lord Mountbatten.

The first Prime Minister of India was Jawaharlal Nehru, a foreign-qualified leader who followed the Western style of democracy but developed the political institution more efficiently than its neighboring counterpart, Pakistan. Contrary to this, China's political layout evolved and was made by the Chinese, not by any English, Dutch, or other foreigners. The policies of Chinese leadership aimed to foster nationalism and growth consensus. In the meantime, policies were not drafted, providing different actors flexibility in different ways.[3]

Both countries have their political differences in Arunachal and Sikkim. It was news in India today, on September 4, 2005, that China and India value each other's friendship and have resolved their border conflict in Sikkim. Defence Minister Pranab Mukherjee said, "On Sikkim and Arunachal Pradesh, we have differences; however, the difference in Sikkim was resolved during the last visit of Chinese Premier Wen Jiabao to India in April."[4] He also said that China has resolved its border disputes with ten other neighboring countries except for Bhutan and India. He thought India was doing its best to have confidence-building measures with China on the issue of Arunachal Paradesh. Parnab Mukherjee called China an invader in the said territory.

In the field of economy, both China and India are following more or less the same tactics for their economic development. They both are trying to capture the international market through dumping. Mr. Sunil said that a stark difference between China and India is that China may have a vibrant economy but remains a feebly justifiable actor in the global sphere. China's deleveraging policies, like its crackdown against excessive bank borrowing and shadow banking, have contributed to attracting more foreign investors.

Additionally, foreign financial institutions are ready to provide loans to a more significant number of Chinese customers. China's new central bank governor intends to allow foreign investments in A-class shares through reforms.[5] We can take this statement of Mr. Sunil as hypothetically correct but not realistically. It is an open secret that in the modern world, the Chinese economy has been consistently rising day by day and sweeping a large amount of growth rate in the world.

He boosts, "India, as the world's largest open society, is ideally poised to step into this opening, as it remains one of the great modernist political successes of the non-Western world and one of the very few that has amassed the political capital of a democratic state which has, to a large degree, respected internal diversity."[6] Another expert talks about India's economic achievements in the following way: Mr. Basu says India's economic achievements remain subject to endless unappealing appraisal with neighboring China, As it seems India is not well ahead of China in evaluating economic indicators, "including growth, per capita income level, consumption of key consumer and food items, social indicators such as life expectancy, literacy, and infant mortality."[7]

China and India are two success stories in the age of globalization. In international media, it has been considered that the twenty-first century is an "Asian century." The Chinese economic think tank opines the same way that it is not a "Chinese Century but an Asian Century." India also has an obsession to go along with China in economic development. There are different opinions on the present condition of the Chinese economy. Some people say that it is a direct outcome of the Chinese adoption of economic liberalization based on and others say that Thus some argue that the recent Chinese economic success is because of liberalization and openness towards the outer world, especially foreign investment. Others say it is because "early Communist history of land reforms and egalitarian policies formed the essential basis upon which all subsequent change has depended."[8]

In the 1980s, diaspora professionals played an essential role in shaping Rajiv Gandhi's reform agenda. However, these diasporas lacked material resources, and their ties were confined to national bureaucrats. On the other hand, the case of Chinese diasporas was different; they had access to a broader range of domestic actors and facilitated the provision of capitalist ideas and material resources.[9]

The literature review of the international political economy gives us a categorical expression about the essential differences between the two economies, which makes such comparison very apparent, and it also gives us a solid argument that the policy of one country may not be applicable for the same purpose to another country. In the case of China and India, we can find ten glaring differences.[10] Jayati Ghosh has explained these differences in his essay published in August 2005.

The first difference depicts the Chinese economy as a command economy with a robust public sector economy. On the other hand, the Indian economy has been a mixed economy with a large private sector. Jayati Ghosh writes in her essay titled *China and India: The Big Differences,* "The Indian economy is a capitalist market economy with the associated tendency to involuntary unemployment. So, the need for macroeconomic policies to stimulate demand, as common in capitalist economies, operated in addition to the usual "developmental" role of the state."[11]

The second difference between the two economies is that China controls the domestic financial sector. In India, the financial sector is neither under the control of the government nor under the private sector. In India, financial liberalization in the 1990s involved progressive deregulation, showing less state intervention in financial affairs. In China, otherwise, the state controls the financial sector even in the process of 'neo-liberalization.' Jayati Gosh says, "Four major public sector banks handle the bulk of the transactions in the economy, and the Chinese authorities have essentially used control over the consequent financial flows to regulate the volume of credit (and therefore manage the economic cycle) as well as to direct credit to priority sectors."

The third difference is the high rate of GDP growth in China compared to the moderate growth in India. Some scholars claim that the Chinese central state was too weak, to the detriment of the national economy. In contrast, other scholars argue that top-down political organizations make local governments weaker than the national authority.[12] The Chinese economy's average annual rate has been 9.8 percent for two and a half decades, while India has had almost 5 to 6 percent per year in the same period.

The higher GDP rate in China relates to the fourth significant difference, which is concerned with a much higher investment rate in the country. "The investment rate in China (investment as a share of GDP) has fluctuated between 35 and 44 percent over the past 25 years, compared to 20 to 26 percent in India."

The fifth difference can be seen from the perspective of economic diversification and structural change. China has followed the classic industrialization pattern, moving from primary to higher manufacturing activities for the last 25 years. The manufacturing sector in China has provided a double workforce and three times more share of output, which has become "the workshop of the world." On the other hand, in India, the development has been from agriculture to services in the share of output. Still, no sizeable increase in manufacturing and employment structure has persistently opposed change.

The sixth glaring difference lies in trade policy and trade patterns.' Chinese export growth has been much more based on aggressive marketing in the world. Besides that, Chinese states have also been interested in providing basic amenities of life like housing, food, and cheap transport facilities, which have reduced labor costs for employers. On the other hand, cheap labor in India is due to poverty, low wages, and weak infrastructure.

> "There is another issue relating to trade policy. In China, the rapid export growth generated employment which was a net addition to domestic employment, since until 2002 China had undertaken much less trade liberalization than most other developing countries. This is why manufacturing employment has proliferated in China. It was not counterbalanced by any loss of employment through the effects of the displacement of the domestic industry because of import competition. This is unlike the case in India, where increases in export employment were outweighed by employment losses especially in small enterprises because of import competition."[13]

Jayati Ghosh finds the seventh difference in poverty reduction. He thinks China is more successful in reducing poverty than India. It is officially declared in China that 4 percent of the people live under the poverty line, while unofficial sources believe this figure is almost 12 percent. In India, people are very much poor. It is considered that 26 to 34 percent of the population in India lives under the poverty line, according to 1999-2000 data. Here on the word is the original text of Jayati Ghosh's views on the difference between China and India:

The Chinese success in this regard can be related to several features. To begin with, the primary issue regarding asset redistribution and basic needs provision was the focus of the Communist state until the late 1970s. This also assisted in economic growth: because of the more egalitarian system, there was a larger mass market for consumption goods, which allowed producers to take advantage of economies of scale. Subsequently, poverty reduction in China has been concentrated into two main phases: 1979-82 and 1994-96, both of which were higher crop prices and rising agricultural incomes. In the first phase, institutional change allowed peasant production in diversified crops, significantly increasing productivity and benefiting peasants from rising prices. Also, since Chinese economic growth has been more employment-generating, this has operated to reduce poverty.

China watchers are generally polarized between two extremes: "Either China will devour the world, or it is on the brink of collapse." Some analyze China's economy within the narrow framework of the Western financial crisis, overlooking the factor of its growing trade with other Asian nations and Europe. Many scholars ignore the government's restructuring efforts and investor demands while remaining confined to state-owned enterprises. China is deeply embedded in the Asian economic system in mutually interdependent ways.[14]

Until recently, there was much more focus on "human development" in China and the public provision of health and education. This included universal education until Class X and better public services to ensure nutrition, health, and sanitation. However, in recent years, this emphasis has been much reduced, and there is greater privatization of such services in China, which has also led to worsening conditions, especially in particular areas. In India, the public provision has been highly inadequate throughout this period and has deteriorated in per capita terms since the early 1990s.

Regarding inequality, the recent growth pattern has been unequal in both economies. The spatial inequalities across regions have been the sharpest in China. Vertical inequalities and the rural-urban divide have become much more marked in India. In China recently, as a response to this, there have been some top-down measures to reduce inequality, for example, through changes in tax rates, more significant public investment in Western and interior regions, and improved social security benefits. In India, a political change has forced more significant attention to redressing inequalities, though the process is still very nascent.

This brings into focus the tenth big difference: that of political systems. It can be argued that the political democracy in India, which now appears deeply entrenched even though it has not translated into universal economic enfranchisement, has played some role in creating more confused but less extreme patterns of economic growth. Indeed, historic and potentially transformative economic legislation such as the Employment Guarantee Act could only come about because of the impact of political changes. Perhaps the ability of the political system to force at least some change of direction in India's economic policies can serve as an essential example to the rest of the world, one of which Indians can justly be proud.

Surprisingly, however, in terms of prospects, both economies end up with similar issues despite these significant differences. There are straightforward questions about the sustainability of China's current economic expansion pattern, based on a high export-high accumulation model that requires constantly increasing shares of world markets and very high investment rates. Similarly, the hope in some policy quarters in India that IT-enabled services can become the engine of growth raises questions of sustainability.

The two economies' most important problems are also similar - the agrarian crisis and the need to generate more employment. In both economies, public intervention has neglected the social sectors recently. In both countries, the policy message appears to be the same: the most essential issues need to be addressed first, and if so, the other areas of expansion will probably look after themselves.

Jayati Ghosh's views are pertinent and hold water in describing such differences unbiased and scientifically. We can deduce from such views that China and India may rise together in the twenty-first century if they assist each other in holding together the whole Asian economy and keeping the Western influence at arm's length. China and India can easily escape the Asian countries from dependentia. They can put an end to neo-colonialism, which has been a characteristic of the developing countries, by carving out the Asian Union. Here are some other differences that have been explained by other Indian Scholars that are exposing the differences in different fields.

The gap between the two countries under discussion is increasing owing to the rapid age of globalization, but in healthy competition, China and India are growing. China has launched the World's first "commercial maglev (magnetic levitation) train between the Pudong International Airport and downtown Shanghai. It takes just seven minutes to cross the 30-kilometer distance- about the same distance between Mumbai's international airport and Nariman Point, which takes anywhere from 75 minutes to a couple of hours to cover."[15]Another difference can be found in sports. At the 2004 Olympics held in Athens, China won 63 medals as compared to one by India.

Coalitional and agitational politics, the backlog of court cases, environmental degradation, democracy, and the rule of law are such attributes of India that have not only delayed the implementation of economic reforms in India for more than a decade but also added significantly to the costs. And the direct cost appreciation is possibly only a tiny part of the total cost to the economy. It can be easily understood that output is lost owing to delays at the start of the project. China started its economic reform process in 1979 while India did it in 1991; therefore, such delay can be considered a genuine reason for all such differences.

Socially speaking, both countries are proud of their legacies. China looks more pragmatic in its cultural outlook, even captured by the Western food chains like McDonald's, KFC, Pizza Hut, etc., as compared to India, where the flow of information has transformed Indian society into an impersonation of the West, not only Western food chains, Banks and MNCs are penetrating successfully in India, but also films of Hollywood gives a different way of communication in Indian masses.

For instance, obscenity is increasing in films in India. It was not in vogue in the last one or two decades of Indian cinemas, but in the twenty-first century, it has become part and parcel of Indian films. However, Bollywood films are screened at international film festivals. It also opens doors to the tourism industry; for example, 2016 Brazilian tourism to India grew eightfold. In addition, many government agencies, like Finland, Israel, and Fiji, offer significant tax rebates to Indian film studios.[16] The producers and directors look inspired by Hollywood movies and never resist shooting bold love scenes. Such obscenity in Chinese films and cinema is still like a once-in-a-blue moon. All these impersonations are de-tracking Indian youth towards nowhere.

Indian television is the worst of all as it attracts more audiences in India, a natural source of 'relative deprivation and 'migration of dreams.' Star Plus is an Indian TV channel that telecasts dramas that are usually based on issues of social degradation in society with makeup and dresses of credits that are not a part of Indian society. Most of the dramas are based on issues of extramarital affairs of spouses, divorce, love marriages, and conspiracies in families. These are not the only subjects in Indian society. Poverty, pollution, inequality, gender discrimination, and religious intolerance are the main issues in India that any Indian TV channel has hardly televised.

Indian films are more critical of its political system than those of China. Chinese TV usually does not criticize government policies. In China, information and communication resources are state-controlled. They never talk against the aspirations of the Chinese government. Analytically speaking, owing to more freedom and democracy, India can take advantage of the communication revolution and do much better things to uplift its society through media. China cannot do that as it is under the thumb of state control media. Corruption is deep-rooted in both societies.

Asia is under transition owing to two big powers, China and India. Both powers are busy restructuring their economic and political systems according to prevailing circumstances. They intend to accompany the globalized world. Asian Tigers like Hong Kong, Singapore, South Korea, and Taiwan are constantly inspired by Japan. China and India are 40% of the world's population that can shake the world. The Chinese economic growth rate is almost 11 %, and India's is 8-9 %, the fastest in the world. Lee Kuan Yew, Former Prime Minister of Singapore, says, "China is the world's factory; India the outsourcing services center first in call centers and now moving to more sophisticated business process operations and clinical research activities of global corporations."[17] He further says that both nations are learning from the developed and developing worlds and trying their best to adopt methods and techniques that may boost their economies in the best way. Here is the original text of that former prime minister's evaluation of China and India.

"I have been deeply interested in China and India since I started my political life in 1950. Like all democratic socialists of the 1950s, I have tried to analyze and forecast which giant would make the grade. I had hoped it would be a democratic India, not a communist China".

By the 1980s, I had become more realistic and accepted the differences. It is simplistic to believe that democracy and free markets are the formulae that must lead to progress and wealth. However, I am convinced the contrary hypothesis is true that central planning and state-owned or nationalized enterprises lead to inefficiency and poor returns, whether the government is authoritarian or democratic. Moreover, even if China and India were democratic, authoritarian, or communist, their performance would differ. I now believe that, besides the standard economic yardsticks for productivity and competitiveness, there are intangible factors like culture, religion, and other ethnic characteristics and national ethos that affect the outcome.

At the start of World War II, China was behind India. China's infrastructure and population were devastated by the Japanese occupation from 1937-45. Then, a civil war followed. After the Communist victory in 1949, China adopted the system of governance and economic policies of the Soviet Union.

At independence in August 1947, India had ample sterling balances, a sound system of governance, and many top-class institutions. It had functioning institutions for democracy, the rule of law, a neutral, highly trained civil service, a defense force, and proficiency in the English language. The 1980s is significant as the Indian upper class began to develop close ties to entrepreneurial relatives in America. The social basis of India's democratic marked changes due to the transnational exchange of diaspora."[18]

The situation deteriorated over time. India adopted central planning with results nearly as damaging as those of China. India's political leaders are determined to reform but the Indian bureaucracy has been slower and resistant to change. Regional jostling and corruption do not help. Furthermore, populist democracy makes Indian policies less consistent, with regular changes in ruling parties. For example, Hangzhou and Bangalore are comparable cities. Hangzhou's new airport opened in 2000; Bangalore has been on the drawing board for years and was only given the go-ahead by the state government in December 2004.

China, the economically backward country in 1950, caught up with India and has surpassed India in several sectors. How did communist China catch up, and why did democratic India lose its lead?

Comparison of the Chinese and Indian Public Sector

Did China pull ahead because it had better governance systems and methods of determining public policies? Tax system. Ten years ago, China had a complicated tax system. There were provincial and municipal sales taxes, border taxes, excise duties, and levies. China has made tax collection efficient and effective by imposing a single value-added tax on manufactured goods.

India had made several unsuccessful attempts to introduce a national VAT, the last on 1st April 2005, when 20 states switched to VAT, but eight are still holding out. Corruption bedevils both, but bureaucratic red tape has lowered India's efficiency and effectiveness more than China's. It takes 88 days to secure all the permits needed to start a business in India, compared to 46 in China. Insolvency procedures take 11 years, as opposed to 2.6 in China. Despite the Great Leap Forward disasters in 1958 and the Cultural Revolution of 1966-76, China pulled itself up after its open-door policy from 1978.

Comparison of the Chinese and Indian Private Sector

India's private sector is superior to China's. Indian companies, although not on par with the best American or Japanese companies because of India's semi-closed market, nevertheless have several near world-class companies, like Tata Consultancy Services, Infosys, and Wipro. Indian multinationals are now acquiring Western companies in their home markets. Moreover, Indian companies follow international corporate governance rules and offer a higher return on equity than Chinese companies. And India has transparent and functioning capital markets.

China has not yet created great companies despite being the third-largest spender in the world on research and development. There has been Chinese corporate fraud on a much larger scale.

What can China and India Learn from each other?

China can learn democratic norms and values from India to make its political system more flexible for the outside world. India is number two in the world regarding information technology after Israel. Therefore, China can enhance relations with India in information technology to speed up its technological advancement in the communication age. Learning English is another passion China has to cope with the contemporary world. They may learn faster than India, even though they may never have been used to it ever before like the Indians, who are good at the English language and its literature. However, the Chinese will have enough English to network easily with business people and scholars in America and Europe. China is following India's technical and technological skills lead and has started supplying software engineers to multinational corporations like Cisco.

India has proliferated over the last decade but has far lower investment rates than China. China must learn to be as efficient as India in utilizing its resources. The Chinese are keen to develop a services sector like India's. For example, they have contracted an Indian company to train 1,000 Chinese software project managers from Shenzhen in etiquette, communications, and negotiation skills. Huawei, a leading Chinese technology company, invested in Bangalore to tap its software skills. The Chinese want to attain international standards for the software outsourcing industry and learn how to deal with US and European clients as India is doing.

India wants to be as successful as China in attracting foreign and domestic investments in manufacturing. India must emulate the practical way China has built up its extensive communications and transportation infrastructure, power plants, and water resources and implemented policies that led to considerable FDIs in manufacturing, high job creation, and high growth. India's spectacular growth has been in IT services, which do not generate high job creation. But it has now drawn up a massive highway construction program over half completed.

Challenges Facing China and India

Parag Khanna claims that even when Western analysts are asked to name and comment on the countries with the most admirable plans and vision, they are more likely to mention China, India, and Singapore. No different is the case of the global general public as a twenty-five-country survey conducted in 2017 ranks India (53 percent) and China (49 percent), which means that both supersede the United States (40 percent) in the context of global positive influence. [19] There is no success like success. Therefore, China and India are determined to enjoy the era of globalization. They must adopt its basics regarding true democratic ideals, human rights, and religious tolerance. Traditional democracies accuse both countries of being subjective towards other communities. India has to bridge the gap between the rural and urban elite; China has to be more pragmatic in the development and incentives of coastal areas. It is still backward and needs attention.

They have to give respect to their neighbors. China should respect the autonomy of Taiwan, Tibet, and Hong Kong. China and India have their specific advantages but face similar challenging social, economic, and political problems. China has to restructure its state-owned enterprises, fix its weak banking sector, and ensure its economy grows fast enough to absorb the still massive army of unemployed. India has poor infrastructure, high administrative and regulatory barriers to business, and large fiscal deficits, especially at the state level, that drag on investment and job creation.

In fifty years, China and the rest of Northeast Asia (Japan, Korea, Taiwan) will be at the high end of the technology ladder. Southeast Asia will mainly be at the lower and middle end of the value-added ladder, with ample opportunities for efficient competitors. On the other hand, India will have certain regions at the high end of the technology ladder, but it may have vast rural areas lagging, like the Russian hinterland during the Soviet era. To avoid this, India has to build up its infrastructure of an expressway across the sub-continent, faster and more railway connections, more airports, expand telecoms and open up its rural areas.

Why are the Chinese Ahead?

The Chinese are more homogeneous: 90% Han, one language and culture, one written script, with varying pronunciations. Having shared a common destiny over several millennia, they are more united as a people. And they can swiftly mobilize resources across the continent for their tasks.

China's Deng Xiaoping started its open-door policy in 1978. In the 28 years since China has more than tripled its per capita GDP. The momentum of its reforms has transformed the lives of its people, thus making its market reform policies irreversible.

India's one billion people are of different ethnic groups with different languages, cultures, and traditions. It recognizes 18 main languages, 844 dialects, and six main religions. India has to make continuous and significant efforts to hold together different peoples who were brought together in the last two centuries into one polity by the British Raj that joined parts of the Mogul empire with the princely states in the Hindi-speaking north and the Tamil, Telegu, and other linguistic/racial groups in the south.

India began liberalizing in 1990. However, India's system of democracy and rule of law gives it a long-term advantage over China, although in the early phases, China has the advantage of faster implementation of its reforms. China develops and becomes a predominantly urban society; its political system must evolve to accommodate a large, better-educated middle class that will be highly educated, better informed, and connected with the outside world, one that expects a higher quality of life in a clean environment and wants to have its views heard by a government that is transparent and free from corruption.

China and India will launch FTA negotiations that may be completed in a few years. Premier Wen Jiabao visited India recently, soon followed by President Hu Jintao. Their closer economy will have a significant impact on the world. ASEAN and Singapore can only benefit from their closer economic links. Many Indians are influential on Wall Street, in US MNCs, the World Bank, IMF, and research institutes and universities. This network will give India an extra edge. China's decision to become a member of WTO was viewed as "raising a white flag"; Both conservatives and liberals of the ruling elite sensed that doomsday was not too far. It was beyond even anyone's imagination that the Chinese economy could go so far.[20] More Chinese are joining this American-based international network but do not yet have the same English language and culture facilities. And because of the Sino-U.S. rivalry, there will be greater reserve when Americans interact with them.

For a modern economy to succeed, a whole population must be educated. The Chinese have developed their human capital more effectively through a nationalized education system. In 1999, 98% of Chinese children had completed five years of primary education, as against 53% of Indian children. India did not have universal education, and educational standards diverged much more sharply than in China. In some states like Kerala, participation in primary schools is 90%. In some states, it is less than 30%. In 2001 India's illiteracy rate was 42%, against China's 14%.

India had many first-rate universities at independence. Except for a few top universities, such as the Indian Institutes of Technology and Indian Institutes of Management, that still rank with the best, it could not maintain the high standards of its many other universities. Political pressures are made for quotas for admission based on caste or connections with MPs.

China has repaired the damage the Cultural Revolution inflicted on its universities. Admission to Chinese universities is based on the entrance examination. China has built a much better physical infrastructure. China has 30,000 km of the expressway, ten times as much as India, and six times as many mobile and fixed-line telephones per 1,000 persons. India must invest massively in its roads, airports, seaports, telecommunications, and power networks to catch up. The current Indian government has recognized this in its budget. It must implement the projects expeditiously.

The Chinese bureaucracy has been organized to adopt best practices in its system of governance and public policies. They have studied and are replicating what Japan, Korea, Taiwan, Singapore, and Hong Kong have done. China's coastal cities are catching up fast. But China's vast rural interior is lagging, exposing severe disparities in wealth and job opportunities. The central government is acutely aware of these dangers. It has dispatched some of the most energetic and successful mayors and provincial governors to these disadvantaged provinces to narrow the gap.

China's response to these looming problems is proactive and multi-faceted. For example, China National Petroleum Corporation and China National Off-shore Oil Corporation (CNOOC) have moved into Indonesian oil and gas fields to meet energy needs. Chinese companies have even gone to Venezuela, Angola, and Sudan. Moreover, ASEAN members' 2025 master plan will harmonize banking, telecoms, and e-commerce standards. Intraregional travel services at affordable prices will also promote tourism and employment.[21]

India signed a recent agreement with Myanmar to import gas by pipeline via Bangladesh. The Indian government plans to consolidate its state-owned oil companies and act proactively like China's CNOOC. The ASEAN-China Free Trade Agreement is an example of China's pre-emptive moves. China moved faster than Japan by opening its agricultural sector to ASEAN countries. India is also negotiating a Closer Economic Cooperation Agreement with ASEAN, but China has gotten there first. (Excerpted from Keynote Speech by Minister Mentor Lee Kuan Yew at the Official Opening of the Lee Kuan Yew School of Public Policy on April 4, 2005).

The excerpts of his interview can be found at the end of the thesis, which has been attached as an appendix. Now, we move towards the ongoing international economic and financial crises and see how they affected China and India.

Current Financial Crisis and its Impact on China and India

It needs proper rules and regulations to sustain its economy on sustainable grounds when any economy wishes to open up itself in the world. In India, it happens otherwise. A country that exceeds more than a billion in population has to think twice while making economic, political, and social decisions. "In a country where 70 % of the population is food-insecure, targeting is both inefficient and iniquitous, as it will tend to exclude a significant part of the food-insecure population."[22]

Poverty is increasing day by day in India. The gap between the rich and the poor is rising, making the political system vulnerable. More than twenty-seven secessionist movements are on the card, but the political elite in India cannot make wise decisions regarding the welfare of the people. How the Indian economy is under pressure in the wake of the ongoing financial and economic crises of the world? The researcher tries to find an answer by making a synthesis based on the lecture of a social scientist, Mr. Venkatesh Athreya, delivered in memory of Uddharaju Ramam, an essential leader of the peasants.

Venkatesh Athreya delivered this lecture in 2009 and admonished the Indian government by furnishing complex realities. He categorically refuted that India remained unharmed by the current financial crisis in the world. He believes they live in a fool's paradise[23] who thinks like that. He opines that the Indian government only invited prominent businessmen and discussed the financial and economic crises with them. It reveals that crony capitalism is still deeply rooted in the economic affairs of Asia. In a democratic country, it is absolutely against morality that a few business tycoons were called for consultation.

At the outset, the Indian government hesitated and resisted accepting any financial crisis. Gradually, it started accepting that India had a liquidity crisis, but in reality, it was a matter of solvency. It means that the Reserve Bank of India (RBI) did its best to give loans to industrialists and other big companies, but they declined the offer. Even other banks were not interested in taking loans from RBI as there was no one to utilize those loans owing to the uncertain market. "The Reserve Bank of India lowered the interest rates at which it lends to banks; it lowered the statutory liquidity ratio (SLR) and the cash reserve ratio (CRR)." This lowering of interest could not attract the borrowers to take out a loan from the bank due to the lopsided market forces (that means supply and demand).

The question is, why was the market so uncertain? The answer is straightforward: When foreign investors were allowed to invest money in the Indian stock market, it rose when the same investors withdrew their money to sustain their economies back home, which crashed the stock market. This is how the world financial crisis influenced the Indian economy. The foreign institutional investors (FIIs) always think about their profits without concern for the local economy. India allowed FIIs without any constraints. It caused an unfavorable trade balance in India as exports were less than imports. This outrightly made an impact on the Indian economy. Indian government must make policies while inviting foreign investors to invest in stock markets that they have to invest for, say, five years or ten years. Still, no visible policy was made that led to the economic crisis in India. The monopoly of foreign investors was creeping up as the Indian government only focused on foreign investment without considering the consequences.

These economic crises are due to India's increasingly integrated economy in the age of globalization. These crises did not prevail in 1991 when the Indian economy was less integrated with the world economy. Outsourcing is a primary reason for India's economic and financial crises. Venkatesh Athreya says that the value of the Indian imports and exports was less than 10% of the GDP in 1991. In 2009, the imports and exports crossed 40 % of the GDP. Therefore, liberalization has made the Indian economy more open to global trade.

It is evident that when a country intends to develop itself according to the international environment, it has to open up its economy accordingly; therefore, it was natural for the Indian economy to be influenced by prevailing financial crises. Besides that, the Indian government spends more on defense than education and health, which have always been top priorities in the West. Spending more on defense is always fruitless as it has been a dead investment. Since no missile, bomb, or tank gives back any economic output or profit that could sustain any world economy. It gives carcasses, injuries, worries, diseases, and deprivations.

After the Indra Gandhi Sikh movement in Punjab to create Khalistan, other insurgencies in India started surging quite rapidly. It shook Indian economic and political instability. These secessionist movements are still happening in India and undermining the socio-political and economic development of the country. Such movements start with a sense of deprivation caused by the unfulfilled dreams of the people of different communities. In such circumstances, these people feel aloof from the system and do not participate in the country's development. This non-participatory character of the people leads the country towards economic and financial crises. Social capital has been a weapon in the hands of developed economies. It works only in integrated societies, not economically deprived and psychologically torn peoples.

In India, the rural and urban political elite could not bridge the gap between leaders, which led to enhanced participation of the people in the political system. Therefore, it caused an imbalance between the core and the periphery. The core was developed with the hard work of the population of the periphery. It enhances deprivation that obliges the periphery to insurgencies. Poverty is another factor that causes deprivation in the masses at the periphery level. It destabilizes the agriculture sector in India.

Ravi Sheth, Great Eastern Shipping Director, stated, "Let's face it. In their heart of hearts, nobody wanted liberalization. It sounded nice, so everyone cheered. Now that it begins pinching you, you cry foul." [24] Venkatesh Athreya shows his concern over two decades of liberalization caused damage in India in five ways. First, the government finished the subsidies in agriculture inputs (fertilizers, pesticides, transport, and other paraphernalia) that raised the exact prices and therefore dented the agricultural sector in India. It is an agricultural country. By capturing its agriculture, its economy can be easily messed up.

This is where Indian policymakers could not figure out that the U.S.-India civil nuclear deal and other such projects assisted the foreigners in weakening the Indian economy in covert action. Second, outsourcing agricultural products without proper rules and regulations lessened the value of Indian products at home. Third, the rising interest rate for agricultural loans depreciates the interest of the farmers. Fourth, with the end of subsidies, agricultural infrastructure in the periphery was weakened. Fifth, the absence of a trickledown effect affected the grassroots level and influenced the economy as a whole. These are the five primary reasons the Indian economy was affected by prevailing economic and financial crises.

Contrary to this, joint ventures are the only way to get into the Chinese system in China, which is why they are less affected by international financial and economic crises than India. Second, China distributed the economic fruits of globalization in all parts of the country to amalgamate every sector for state and national development. Moreover, China's foreign strategies in the form of CGG and BRI have more significant implications for inside China, too. These global projects integrate the international actors and allow local governments and markets to promote their economic and entrepreneurial plans.[25] It developed core areas and periphery and injected fiscal stimulus in agricultural and rural areas efficiently to bridge the gap between urban and rural sectors. Although the researcher cannot deny China's socio-economic and political inequalities, they can only be perceived more in coastal and far-flung rural areas. It does not damage the Chinese economy very much. Indeed, it caused deprivations among a few people, as Xinjiang, the capital of Urumqi, was affected by recent ethnic riots, but China managed to control it effectively.

The Chinese people are participating more efficiently in the country's development than India; therefore, it gets more economic fruits; this participatory character of Chinese social capital is a natural source of their sustainable economic development. Proper rules and regulations for foreign MNGs restrict their influence in China. Consequently, it finishes the threat of MNG monopoly.

The Asian States forges a new geometry of cooperation. Today, major regional powers, India, Japan, and Vietnam, stand up to China to take pride in their history and claim sovereignty. Besides military cooperation, Asian solidarity is shown by providing shelter and protecting their neighbors against the most nefarious militant groups.[26]

China's trade balance has been very favorable for the last three decades; it exports more than imports. This is the key to Chinese success, rather than keeping it away from ongoing economic and financial crises. It is hard to believe that China remained altogether unaffected by these international financial crunches as its environment was damaged heavily; as mentioned in the second chapter, China was emitting carbon dioxide almost 14 %, the second highest after the U.S. therefore, environmental degradation in China is happening to owe to the increased competition in the international market.

The demand for Chinese consumer products is much higher compared to any other country in the world. Besides that, China is busy making synthetic products. For example, Apple is an American Macintosh brand, but the iPhone from Apple is made in China. Toshiba is a Japanese company, but Toshiba's laptops are made in China.

Therefore, China seems to be a significant source of international economic and financial crises, pushing other economies into the corner. It may be a temporary phase of Chinese development as imitation cannot be sustained longer. This is where China is being affected unknowingly, owing to fulfilling the needs and demands of the world's people on a large scale without quality but with quantity. It may collapse its economy after two decades or so since human beings are always quality-conscious. Thus, both China and India are affected by ongoing international financial and economic crises but in different ways.

In September, two months before hosting the G20 summit meeting in November 2009, the Obama administration adopted a protectionist policy by increasing the tariffs on Chinese tires by 35 percent to save the local tire industry. It is criticized by the Chinese commerce ministry and considered against world trade rules. The United States International Trade Commission demands levying duties up to 55 percent.[27] This is all due to world economic crises. The U.S. is facing unemployment at home and is obliged to put duties on imported goods. Thus, China suffered from this world economic crunch. It shocked the traders. The Chinese Ministry of Commerce has decided to raise this issue in the forthcoming G20 summit meeting.

Therefore, even with efficient system capabilities, sometimes circumstances put the country in an unavoidable situation. It does not mean system capabilities are no longer critical; natural happening is more important. Thus, seeking a solution to every problem in political, economic, and social domains is impossible. In unforeseen circumstances, natural calamities may occur without any storm, hurricane, earthquake, or flood. Such exogenous factors have no physical existence but play an essential role in determining the international political economy. Conceding this fact, we move towards the conclusion and findings of the study.

Endnotes

1 Oded Shenkar, *The Chinese Century: The Rising Chinese Economy and Its Impact on the Global Economy, the Balance of Power, and Your Job,* Pennsylvania: Wharton School Publishing, 2005, 55.

2 Ibid., 55-56.

3 Min Ye, *The Belt Road, and Beyond State-Mobilized Globalization in China: 1998-2018*: Cambridge University Press, 2020,113.

4 http://news.indiainfo.com/2005/09/04/0409china-pranab-arunachal.html visited on 26-12-07.

5 Parag Khanna, *The Future is Asian: Commerce, Conflict, and Culture in the 21st Century*: Simon & Schuster, 2019, 154.

6 Sunil Khilnani, India as a Bridging Power, published in 2005 by The Foreign Policy Centre, 49 Chalton Street London.

7 Prasenjit K. Basu, India, and the Knowledge Economy: The "Stealth Miracle" is Sustainable, published in 2005 by The Foreign Policy Centre 49, Chalton Street London.

8 http://macroscan.org/cur/aug05/cur240805China_India.htm visited on 26-12-07.

9 Min Ye, *Diasporas and Foreign Direct Investment in China and India*: Cambridge University Press, 2014, 87.

10 Ibid.

11 Ibid.

12 Min Ye, *The Belt Road and Beyond: State-Mobilized Globalization in China: 1998-2018*: Cambridge University Press, 2020,173.

13 Ibid.

14 Parag Khanna, *The Future is Asian: Commerce, Conflict, and Culture in the 21st Century*: Simon & Schuster, 2019, 137.

15 A.V. Rajwade, India and China: a January 18, 2005 comparison. http://www.rediff.com/money/2005/jan/18guest.htm Website visited on 26-12-07.

16 Parag Khanna, *The Future is Asian: Commerce, Conflict, and Culture in the 21st Century*: Simon & Schuster, 2019, 314.

17http://www.newasiaforum.org/managing_globalisation_India_and_China.htm visited on 26-12-07.

18 Min Ye, *Diasporas and Foreign Direct Investment in China and India*: Cambridge University Press, 2014, 89.

19 Parag Khanna, *The Future is Asian: Commerce, Conflict, and Culture in the 21st Century*: Simon & Schuster, 2019,254-255.

20 Min Ye, *The Belt Road, and Beyond: State-Mobilized Globalization in China: 1998-2018*: Cambridge University Press, 2020,204.

21 Parag Khanna, *The Future Is Asian: Commerce, Conflict, and Culture in the 21st Century*:

Simon & Schuster, 114.

22 http://www.pragoti.org/node/2948. Website accessed on 25-08-09.

23 Ibid.

24 Min Ye, *Diasporas and Foreign Direct Investment in China and India*: Cambridge University Press, 2014, 128-129.

25 Min Ye, *The Belt Road, and Beyond: State-Mobilized Globalization in China: 1998-2018*: Cambridge University Press, 2020,174.

26 Parag Khanna, *The Future is Asian: Commerce, Conflict, and Culture in the 21st Century*: Simon & Schuster, 131.

27 The Dawn Lahore, Sunday, September 13, 2009, 17.

Chapter 5. Battling Covid-19: A Comparative Analysis between China and India

Covid-19: Myth or Reality

This chapter will compare the two countries, China and India, and how their leadership utilizes their system capabilities to fight COVID-19. The coronavirus disease has speedily developed as a pandemic.[1] Due to its extensive casualties, COVID-19 was a calamity for the global community's health and the international political economy. A mysterious case of pneumonia appeared in Wuhan City in Hubei Province, in China, on December 30, 2019. The instrumental activator was recognized as a new coronavirus in 2019, and the disease was named COVID-19 by the World Health Organization (WHO) on January 7, 2020.[2] The tragedy and extremity of this disease exacerbated the fatality of other health issues, such as patients with cancer, heart disease, depression, hypertension, and lung disease, affected more than any other patient. The whole world started suffering in all domains from this pandemic.[3]

The virus intensified extensively in China's Wuhan region, reaching more than 190 countries and regions. However, scientists started investigating whether the virus transferred from animals to humans or not, though there are multiple controversial reports on the origination of the virus. Since, at that stage, no treatment or cure for the virus was available. Therefore, scientists thought that any patient with coronavirus needs to quarantine, isolate himself, and follow a hygienic environment. The virus has had a vital social and economic effect worldwide.[4] Does the question arise whether this Coronavirus is a myth or a reality?

However, this is taken as a myth by a different group of people from different territories of the globe. Some claimed that the virus originated from bats. It is also suspected to have erupted and spread from Huanan's wholesale seafood market in Wuhan city. In the Journal of Medical Virology, a published article made the first claim that viruses erupted from the snakes. A second claim was that the virus appeared from pangolins, and there are strong possibilities that this virus began from bats. Many experts and evidence identified that Coronavirus had naturally originated in bats. There were different claims that bats instigated severe acute respiratory syndrome and Middle East respiratory syndrome—however, this detrimental virus blowout from animals to homo sapiens.[5]

More than one-third of the globe's population is under some limitations.

China, India, the USA, France, the UK, and Italy have applied the biggest and most constraining mass quarantines, emergency protocols that mainly stop people from departing a zone (Lockdown). In the official magazine of the United Nations, WHO suggested that there is no other way except to go for social distancing and lockdowns in the country were essential to confront the coronavirus. Multiple myths around COVID-19 are making rounds on social media. One of the vital myths is that COVID-19 cannot be transferred via flies. Covid-19 can be transferred via droplets of the infected individual.

It was considered that droplets caused transmission when an individual came into close connection with another individual and also depended upon the individual's varied physiology and anatomy. Not all individuals get the droplet transmission. For example, breathing vociferously might cause virus transmission, but necessarily depending upon the body resistance of the individual who received the droplets. Second, transmission of COVID-19 was not possible in humid and hot climates. It wasn't a myth that this virus could not sustain humid and hot temperatures and would expire. Therefore, cautions regarding social distancing, washing hands frequently, and wearing masks were universally adopted to keep this virus at arm's length. Many other myths had no authenticity or were supported by the WHO.

The most efficient way to avoid this virus was washing with hand soap and water or regularly disinfecting with a practical hand decontaminator. The measures adopted at the international airports were ineffective because thermal scanners at airports were unable to detect coronavirus as thermal scanners are usually utilized to distinguish temperature or people with more noteworthy than average body illness. We found COVID-19 symptomless in many cases and identified diversified reasons for human fever. One of the myths is that antibiotics protect individuals from Coronavirus. However, there are no such antibiotics to treat this virus; though doctors today use it as a preventive element of care, it cannot be used as a way of treatment and prevention. Another claim was that mixing black pepper with honey and garlic syrup prevents Coronavirus. However, no appropriate indication or research proves such claims; honey and garlic still have some disinfectant that might not prevent COVID-19.

Another claim was that the regular use of garlic with salt water foils this virus. Salt water gargling is good for throat infections and cannot prevent the virus. The rumor was that Coronavirus could affect older adults more quickly than young people. The WHO suggests that all age groups should adopt safety measures. However, people with old age and a medical history of asthma, diabetes, and coronary illness are speedily endangered to be extremely ill.[6] As far as reality is concerned, COVID-19 is a severe kind of disease that has cost many lives, and still, people are dying from this virus.

China fights back with COVID-19

China's President Xi Jinping led the nation efficiently and utilized all possible means to protect people from this deadly virus. He successfully created deterrence and control against COVID-19. After the eruption of COVID-19, the government of China gave first preference to battle against the virus and placed the people's lives and health before everything. The open-war period direct system and the policies constructed regarding the ground facts presented potential leadership. The government of China has sustained the concept of depending on the people and observed keeping them well aware of COVID-19 as a significant aspect of constructing relationships between the public and the government.

The pliable and civilized social management and non-medical engagement spotlighted by quality quarantine tools significantly increased the virus. Screening, tests, administrative tools, and epidemiological analysis were demonstrated to be vital in disconnecting the string of virus transmission. By adjusting hospitals focused on helpfulness, transforming patients and the treatments they acquired based on their situations, and amalgamating conventional Chinese medicine into remedies, China strongly reduced the contamination and casualty rates and simultaneously increased the recovery rate.

However, China thoroughly used its social system's benefits, assigned highly effective resources across the state, and protected much-required logistics holdups. As the nation attempts to fight the war and keep Hubei and Wuhan safe, China has created inceptive achievements in deterrence and holding off the virus. Focused on its national condition, China has investigated a set of practices and tools in the control and protection of diseases and also the patient's treatments.[7]

There are six steps and tools that China adopted and has achieved in the battle against the coronavirus:

1. Universal agreement and public marshaling: This includes timely information emancipation, spreading knowledge about control and avoidance, public opinion instruction and media holdup, and universal contribution to social unity.

2. Social isolation and traffic control include city lockdown and transport preservation in hardest-hit zones, converted traffic controls in less acute zones, strategies to avoid social meetings, cross-contamination, and community isolation as a fundamental line of defense.

3. The third is testing, screening, and dynamic watching, which includes in-depth screening in groups, better virus testing, developing a vigorous management system, escalating epidemiological examination, and controlling four communities for specific therapy.

4. Fourth are treatment methods and scientific research, which include dual

objectives of holding the source of contamination, expanding treatment, and improving treatment plans and techniques.

5. Fifth is the allotment of resources and warranty of supplies, which includes Hubei getting a national health workforce brace. Enormous attempts were made in medical supply buildings to harmonize the allotment of daily essentials.

6. Sixth is a direct system and strategic policies containing the highest decision-making procedure, basic policies and strategies, effective implementation apparatus, and thorough counter steps.[8]

Wuhan City, the pivot of the pandemic, is also the main transport center of China's transference system, which links many regions in China. However, new features and changes have doubtlessly placed forward new needs and challenges for the government to counter the COVID-19 epidemic. The government of China has taken significant all-inclusive and national reaction estimates in the battle against the widespread COVID-19 and has gained positive outcomes. The government adopted some main elements to overcome the challenge of the COVID-19 pandemic.

For example, the exigency control estimates of pandemic areas, as COVID-19 has extremely distracted the economy of China and slowed down its business activities for which numerous measures are applied under these destructive circumstances, various enterprises, mainly small and medium-sized companies with enfeeble ability to control the risks are facing many difficulties due to the lack of funds and employees. For this, the Chinese government has presented various strategies to support the survival and establishment of these companies during the pandemic. The companies' funding costs have decreased, reflecting the reality that banks decreased companies' loan doorsteps, escalated loan amounts, and decreased loan interest rates during the pandemic.

Companies severely affected by the pandemic could implement various tax reliefs, and the government also extended its favor in the form of special funds to give subsidy aid to most affected industries, e.g., transportation and aviation. Companies' employees who were back to work from other regions have also received substantial aid from the government and were given subsidies for chartered buses and airplanes.

Fortunately, several national and international companies pooled substantial money and medical tools to the pandemic-affected zones; for example, the Chinese National Petroleum Corporation transferred production lines to deliver medical shielding apparatus with masks, ventilators, and safety clothing.

People started quarantining and calculating the effects of the virus, which became the most vital part of citizen efficiency and awareness against the virus.

Most zones across mainland China have applied the so-called "grid closed management" on a community basis. The campaign against the virus was aggressive in China, and people were restricted to their homes and warned not to go out unnecessarily. The education sector was advised to postpone their academic sessions for the time being without further delay. The Chinese Ministry of Education circulated to all public and private sector universities, schools, and colleges to close by January 27, 2020.

For the safety of the people, all the educational institutions were instructed / advised to use the internet and digital technology to carry on their educational skills and learning and teaching practices online rather than physical or face-to-face sessions. Numerous universities also demonstrated vital initiatives in taking social duties, beginning education platforms for society without charge, sharing good-quality course means, and, in such ways, participating in virus protection and pandemic control.

The pandemic was affecting every aspect of human life. By January 20, 2020, the entire transportation system in China was at respite. Airports, railway stations, and bus terminals were all under surveillance, and no one was allowed to enter or leave the city without proper tests and examination of the human body regarding Coronavirus. Chinese leadership made special arrangements to mitigate the adversaries of the crises by eliminating taxes on express highways by February 17, 2020. These steps were taken to decrease the cost of raw materials and other paraphernalia to secure emergency transportation for the company's reopening. Since March 2020, all international flights have been directed to adopt safety measures after landing in any major cities in China. All the workers were forced to consider COVID-19 a severe threat and quarantine for 14 days at the regional designated isolated points.

The Chinese administration did its best to control the transportation and other relevant resources to confine the virus instead of the free fall spread of its second wave.[9] The Chinese government effectively took pragmatic measures to contain the first coronavirus outbreak prevalent in Wuhan and the surroundings of the Hubei area. The main objective was to control the infection, stop transference, and prevent the spread of the virus.

The proactive method began with cross-sectoral participation in combined prevention and control estimates. Public markets were shut down, and efforts were made to make people aware of the zoonotic disease. On January 03, 2020, information on the pandemic was shared with the WHO, and the WHO was informed of the whole genetic series of COVID-19 on January 10. Agreements for COVID-19 analysis and treatment, monitoring, epidemiologic examination, regulation of close relationships, and laboratory testing were put together, and related monitoring activities and epidemiologic examinations were managed. Investigative testing kits were established, live poultry markets and wildlife were set under unadulterated management, and estimates of the Virus infection were measured.

In the second wave of the coronavirus, the fundamental approach was to diminish the epidemic's severity and lessen the risk of increased causalities. In Wuhan and other significant areas of Hubei, the influx of patients efficiently attended to and provided with medicine in time to avoid deaths and minimize exportations. In other areas, the emphasis was on shielding against any virus import, fighting the virus's spread, and applying protection and control measures together.

The animal markets, where wildlife was commercially sold out, shut down countrywide. The birds or relevant animals were captivated and quarantined with facilities. On January 20, 2020, COVID-19 was incorporated in the reported and border health quarantine infectious diseases, with temperature checks, healthcare claims, and quarantine against COVID-19. On January 23, Wuhan imposed unembellished traffic restrictions. The treatment, diagnosis, pandemic protection, and control agreements were ameliorated; cases of isolation and treatment were expanded.

Measures fixated on safeguarding all cases and close relationships were observed and placed under medical monitoring. It was also realized that people must restrict their movements further, try to keep social distancing and refrain from using public transport to move around. Information regarding the epidemic and preventive measures were regularly circulated. The risks of public interactions and health education were disseminated. The allotment of medical supplies was organized, new hospitals were constructed, preserved beds were utilized, and related buildings were reused to ensure that all infected cases could be treated; attempts were made to keep a stable supply of products and their prices to ensure the smooth functioning of society.

The third wave of the pandemic concentrates on lessening the mass of infected cases, continuously controlling the pandemic, and ensuring a balance between pandemic protection and control of sustainable economic and social progress, the united order, systematized instruction, and scientific evidence-based strategy application. For Wuhan and prime zones of Hubei Province, the attention is on the treatment of the patient and the intervention of transportation, focusing on tangible steps to apply relevant measures for testing, admitting patients, and providing treatment to all patients.

All provinces assisted Wuhan and other hotspots in Hubei Province in resisting the virus's rapid spread and provided appropriate medical aid. Health and welfare services were gradually given to returning employees. Knowledge regarding disease protection is famous for better public health literacy and skills, and a complete program of emergency scientific research is being executed to establish diagnostics, therapeutics, and vaccines, describe the variety of the disease, and realize the source of the virus.[10]

Some states have initiated and planned to apply contact-tracing apps to discover the increasing risks of COVID-19 worldwide. Now, the question arises of how China tackles the pandemic- no full stop. Which tools, measures, policies, and digital technologies are used by China to tackle and control this widespread disease? Regarding China, the government depends on the health code established by Alipay and WeChat to recognize people possibly exposed to COVID-19.

The color-based code could control people's unveiling dangers and liberty of movement based on aspects such as traveling history, the period spent in dangerous regions, and connections to likely transporters. Digital tenets are major players managing health surveillance and moderating state-citizen connections in China. More vitally, tracing apps might appear to be a standard implementation in numerous countries, recommending that aims be considerably acquired for health observation.[11] The eruption of COVID-19 has resulted in a worldly unparalleled reaction to health observation. More than 47 countries have applied contact-tracing apps to suppress the pandemic.[12] (Cohen, 2020).

At the core of the rising Health Code is the performance of digital platforms. Plan of action is a vital player in social and economic relationships. They ease multifaceted markets and enlarge their services into the network. Three players are involved in the Health Code: governments, digital manifesto, and end-users (like citizens). Firstly, the Health Code is an example of China's latest investment in the platform ecosystem. Health Code is based on two commercial principles: one is that the governments permit technology giants to control significant data sources.

However, local governments have liberated administrative viewpoints and regulations to advance and normalize the use of the Health Code, though Alipay and WeChat could share data with local police. Thus, state actors have become important developers and participants in the digital manifesto. Also, the Health Code signals that governments and technology have gained matchless cooperation for pursuing individuals. Secondly, digital platforms were central gatekeepers in the data flows. Also, WeChat and Alipay had sneaked into China's manifesto ecosystem and generated organizational dependencies; hence, citizens (end users) and announcers appear to rely upon these two tenets.

Moreover, the governments depend primarily on a manifesto to collect data and link with citizens. It is vital to note that the Health Code focuses on privacy, security, and accuracy. Presently, the system is chiefly conflicting at local levels.[13]

India Fights Back With COVID-19

As far as India is concerned, it is suffering through this pandemic and is facing a massive loss of lives and infrastructure. India has nearly one-fifth of the globe's population and is the second leading state regarding population. India donates greatly to the globe's GDP and is among the most prominent developing states with robust economic growth percentages.

However, the COVID-19 pandemic outbreak in the Indian zone is being seriously observed and examined by the World, and complete analytical studies focused on multiple policies considered by Indian administrators are occasionally required. India has been following a national lockdown since 22 March 2020. Due to this virus, India is going through the worst situation, and all international and domestic travel has been banned. India is in the third wave of the COVID-19 pandemic, and the cases are increasing continuously.[14]

In India, the cruelest month of COVID-19 is in the world record as daily infected cases crossed an extraordinary 4,00,000 on April 30, 2021. In contrast, a shocking 6.9 million new infections were discovered in the country in the same month. The second wave of Coronavirus infections has created destruction in India, leaving millions of people suffering from this virus and placing stress on the country's already overtaxed health and medical care system.[15]

India has been confronting the Covid-19 battle with a strong political will. Indian Prime Minister Narendra Modi has ensured resolution and firmness in managing the pandemic. The strategic reaction of India to the virus was highly onward in implementing actions selecting central extents as a decree under the International Health Regulations (IHR), much before the eruption was claimed as a Public Health Emergency of International Concern by the World Health Organization. The efforts have been motivated and preventative.[16]

India has followed five approaches in battling COVID-19.
1. Keep going with continual condition awareness.
2. Proactive and Preventative approach.
3. Arranged reaction as per constantly developing framework.
4. Cross-sectorial coordination on every level.
5. Generating a people's development to battle this virus.

India set about the observation of flying from COVID-19 pretentious states twelve days prior. India even had its first coronavirus case on January 30, 2020. The severity of India's estimates is evident in the rigor score given by Oxford University to multiple states as part of an in-progress study that examines the reaction of the governments of numerous countries to the COVID-19 condition. India is one of the very few states that was given an outcome of 100 sudden during the circumstances.

The Indian government has taken essential steps with the developing scenario of Covid-19. To battle Covid-19, social distancing is one of the foremost measures considered by countries. India has been restricted as more prepared per indication of average all-inclusive world health security outcome 2019.

The Union Cabinet, directed by the Prime Minister, Shri Narendra Modi, accepted Indian Rupee (INR) 15,000 crore for the "India Covid-19 Emergency Response and Health System Preparedness Package". The capital (funds) authorized would be used in three phases. For instance, in the COVID-19 Emergency Response, Rs. 7,774 crores have been provided, and the remaining is for medium-term support that would be given under a mission mode perspective.

The government of India and the WHO jointly expanded to overcome the COVID-19 issues. Today, India is facing shortages in medical supplies regarding the health care system and hence cannot tackle the spread of the virus. As the number of infected cases is increasing daily in the state, India's healthcare system needs to make efforts, and genuine training should be given to the healthcare employees to treat the infected people. Undoubtedly, COVID-19 has vitally disturbed the educational sector, which is the state's economic future. Many students from India desire to study in international universities; if this pandemic continues, the demand for abroad education might decrease.

The most significant concern is the consequence of disease on the employment rate. Instant measures must be taken to advance online education in schools and universities in India. An instant measure is needed to reduce the effects of COVID-19 on internship programs, inclusive job offers, and research projects. Furthermore, lockdown with some relaxations requires staying in India long to win against the COVID-19 pandemic. Because of the lockdown, industries, factories, and workplaces are closed, which leads to the misery of numerous daily wage earners and several migrant employees. Hundreds and thousands of employees are getting back to their native places disappointedly.[17]

Covid-19 and its impact on the Political Economies of China and India

Economically, China will likely experience more significant difficulty than other states from the pandemic because of the trade war pressure.[18] Due to the emergence of this harmful disease in China, the situation has presented itself very aggressively in history. The policies China adopted to control this virus were initially a national approach that advanced complete temperature observation, face masking, and hand washing. Therefore, Covid-19 has seriously affected China's political and economic slabs.

As the pandemic developed and knowledge was raised, a scientific and risk-based approach was followed to prevent this disease. Particular controlling measures were fixed to the country, provincial, and interactive context. However, the basic rules of this policy have been agreed upon since its beginning; particular features have been continuously refined to include new knowledge on COVID-19, this virus, and its control as quickly as that knowledge has appeared.

The outstanding speed with which China's scientists and public health experts separated the causative virus, developed diagnostic principles, and determined major transportation frameworks like the path of spread and development time, given the critical evidence base for China's policy, acquiring crucial time for the reaction. Individually, the people of China have responded to this pandemic with bravery and judgment. They have received and attached to the evidence of restraint measures, either the interruption of public get-togethers, staying at home for some months, or restrictions on travel. China's striking approach to controlling the coronavirus's quick spread has altered the course of a rapidly increasing and severe pandemic.

Currently, China is trying to boost its economy, reopen its educational institutions, and return to the normal situation of society. However, a scientific-based, risk-based, and phased approach is being considered with an explicit identification and readiness of the requirement to respond instantly to any new COVID-19 cases or masses as the main aspects of the controlled strategy are raised. Fifty thousand infected cases of COVID-19 are still under clinical treatment in China.

As China is trying to reopen a more normal degree of social and economic activities, the world must identify and respond positively to the quickly altering and reducing the common danger of COVID-19 in China. China's quick return to broad linking with the globe and its complete productive capacity and economic output is crucial to China and the globe. The world community instantly requires access to China's experience reacting to COVID-19 and the material products it brings to the world's response.[19]

The impact of COVID-19 on India's economy was worse than China's. There were two phases of that impact: short and long-term. The short term refers to the financial year 2020-2021, whereas the latter refers to the five years from 2020-2021 to 2024 to 2025. However, 2020-2021 would be recalled as a testing time for the Indian people when their lives looked like they had reset and refurbished. Their economy was troubled, and how it would recover remained a puzzle for most individuals.[20]

Indian economy is part of the world economy; therefore, the international impact has been considered first. Five severe economic aspects, such as GDP growth, inflation, interest rate, unemployment, and industrial output, help measure the impact. Since the blow-up of COVID-19, analysts all over the world have been predicting numerous economic problems for the international economy.

The new calculations exhibit a dimmer image with every transitory day than in previous years. According to the UN, the expected growth of 2.55 was predicted during the fiscal year of 2020, but it had been transferred into a lopsided global growth decreased to 1%. The net impact that is predicted was almost 3.5%. In 2017, the size of the global economy was reduced to $2.8 trillion from $80 trillion after the $3.5 trillion cut-off. It damaged the fifth largest economy, India, very severely.[21]

The dangerous cycle leading to the economic crisis has set on a spin. Falling prices, cut-off supply, lower consumption, lower spending, and job issues all fit in this pandemic era. "A significant impact of COVID-19 is expected on the Indian economy for fiscal 2020–2021. Amid much uncertainty, a positive view can be taken that a recovery will be initiated from the second quarter of 2020– 2021. The recovery will happen in phases and gradually.

The damage recovery depended upon controlling or containing the pandemic in India. Containing COVID-19 was a risk for newly opening-up economies like India and China, which took a heavy toll on both countries' economies. It was the six-month term of the fiscal year of 2020-2021. But it was unimaginably worse in controlling the damage.[22]

Except for oil imports, the world economic crisis does not endanger India's economy. It has its national demand and supply network that could bring back growth rates by 7 to 8 %. Robust political leadership exists at the hub, and the whole performance is substantial in hours of crisis. Analysts recommend that the government of India follow a two-way approach to dealing with the economic crisis. It would improve its industrial sector, which would help boost the country's economy.

One is that this would engage critical contributions from the commercial banks, the central bank, financial institutions, and other agencies in negotiating strategies per the demand of the condition. Second, it would have to drive and include the general public and private companies in reacting to the condition (Barbate, Gade & Raibagkar,2021). "The trade impact of the coronavirus epidemic for India is estimated to be about 348 million dollars, and the country figures among the top 15 economies most affected by COVID-19, according to a UN report. According to the Asian Development Bank (ADB), the Covid-19 outbreak could cost the Indian economy between $387 million and $29.9 billion in personal consumption losses."[23]

There are five main reasons why the national lockdown would be tough to end. Firstly, the increased rate of infected cases is constantly escalating. Secondly, the increase two-fold in the number of infected cases in India is decreasing quickly, creating an active spread. Thirdly, many Indians are pursuing social distances very honestly, with transportability rates moving down for public areas in India.

This is because of the joint attempts of the administrative authorities, combined activities by the Prime Minister, and citizens who would stay away from social incidents. Fourthly, the urgent mass events are destroying the efforts of the Indian authorities to control the spread of Covid-19.

Lastly, the sticking of the people infected from the religious incidents has been extensive in India currently. However, in the last three months, March, April, and May 2021, much tension appeared in India due to the spread of the infected population, and the numbers are increasing with each passing day. It is a very miserable situation in India due to this virus, where a large number of populations lost their lives. Such extreme situations due to COVID-19 have harmed India's political and economic aspects. It slows down its economic activities, lowers social activities, and creates issues among political parties (Gupta, Pal & Pandey, 2020).

Conclusion

To control this global disease, China has expanded its scientific research and presented assistance to other states. China has arranged bilateral combined prevention and control tools with other states, moved ahead in global cooperation, worked jointly with the global community, taken serious attempts and responsibility to protect global public health security, and controlled the spread of the virus globally.

China took the most agile, aggressive, and ambitious measures in reaction to the public health incident, gained a big deal in controlling and blocking the transportation of the pandemic among human beings, and gave helpful experience for the scientific globe and the world community. In the beginning, India's strategy of micro identification, population isolation, and rapid treatment gained portions in protecting against big-scale spread and deaths because of COVID-19.

China and India should maintain a suitable level of emergency organization protocols, relying on the evaluated risk in each region and identifying the real danger of new cases and masses of COVID-19 as economic activity restarts, movement limitations rise, and educational institutions reopen, both the states should make careful restrictions to control the virus and public and gathering places should be properly checked for the prevention of the people.

Regarding essential measures to battle the political and economic impact of the speedily spreading Coronavirus, Indian policymakers would need to apply a vital targeted fiscal, more expansive monetary stimulus, and policy rate penetration to assist the economic condition. As the COVID-19 crisis keeps expanding, producers and manufacturers may face challenges in multiple areas. Manufacturers would also need to view beyond their economic practicability. However, the Indian government is taking all the primary precautions to tackle the pandemic and seek to reduce the spread of this virus.

The government of India is using artificial intelligence through technology, such as by placing the Aarogya Setu App, which assists in generating awareness regarding infection and infection areas more dominantly. However, India is experiencing many problems in the economy, education, corporate, transportation, and healthcare areas.

Controlling COVID-19 may take some months, but public health interventions would be moved towards social distancing and alleviating its effects on public services. Vaccination against COVID-19 has become necessary for every citizen in China and India. China is one of the leading countries to export the vaccine to other states, including India. Vaccination is the sole step to reduce the number of infected patients and fight the pandemic successfully. Vaccination, the use of masks, and social distancing are measures that all communities across the globe should take to counter this disease. Strict implementation and development of measures for health collaboration on an international level are vital in decreasing the threat of COVID-19.

Endnotes

1 Sasbou, L.et.al, COVID 19 Myocarditis: Myth or Reality? *Journal of the Saudi Heart Association*, (2020), *32*(3), 421. Retrieved from https://www.ncbi.nlm.nih.gov/pmc/articles/PMC7721458/, visited on 31-10-2021.

2 Raghuvir, K., Anila, A., Pawan, G. N., Jayesh, M., & Krishnadas, N, COVID-19: Emergence, Spread, Possible Treatments, and Global Burden. *Frontiers in public health*, (2020), *8*, 216.

3 Roy, S., COVID-19 reinfection: myth or truth? *SN Comprehensive Clinical Medicine*, *2*(6), (2020), 710-713.

4 Raghuvir, et.al. 2020.

5 Schneier, B., *Schneier on security*. John Wiley & Sons, (2009).

6 Khan, M. G., Yezdani, U., Chakravorty, A., & Shukla, T., Efforts and Challenges paved by India to confront Corona Virus (COVID-19). *Bangladesh Journal of Medical Science*, (2020), 88-S.

7   (http://www.chinadaily.com.cn/pdf/2020/Chinas.Fight.Against.COVID-19-0420-final-2.pdf).

8   (http://www.chinadaily.com.cn/pdf/2020/Chinas.Fight.Against.COVID-19-0420-final-2.pdf)

9 Liu, W., Yue, X. G., & Tchounwou, P. B. (2020). Response to the COVID-19 epidemic: The Chinese experience and implications for other countries.

10 https://www.who.int/docs/default-source/coronaviruse/who-china-joint-mission-on-covid-19-final-report.pdf.

11 Liang, F., <? covid19?> COVID-19 and Health Code: How Digital Platforms Tackle the Pandemic in China. *Social Media+ Society*, (2020), *6*(3), 2056305120947657.

12 Cohen, D, *Surviving Lockdown: Human Nature in Social Isolation*. (2020), Routledge.

13 Liang, 2020.

14 Gupta, R., Pal, S. K., & Pandey, G, A comprehensive analysis of the COVID-19 outbreak situation in India. (2020), *MedRxiv*.

15 Siddiqui, S. (2021). Covid19 Crisis in India: Situation Beyond Heartbreaking. A Brief Report on Covid-19 Crisis in India. *Ariel Foundational International (AFI)*.

16 Kharb, P. Kapoor, V & Madan, N, Combating Covid-19: The India initiatives. International Journal of Community Medicine and Public Health. (2020), Retrieved from http://dx.doi.org/10.18203/2394-6040.ijcmph20203519.

17 (Khan et al., 2020).

18 (Raghuvir, et.al, 2020).

19   (https://www.who.int/docs/default-source/coronaviruse/who-china-joint-mission-on-covid-19-final-report.pdf).

20 Barbate, V., Gade, R. N., & Raibagkar, S. S., COVID-19 and Its Impact on the Indian Economy. *Vision*, (2021), *25*(1), 23-35.

21 Barbate, Gade & Raibagkar, 2021.

22 Ibid.

23 Koshle, H., Kaur, R., & Basista, R., Breakdown of Business and Workers in India: Impact of Corona Virus. (2020).

Chapter 6. Conclusion

Globalization is a reality in the twenty-first century. It is a matter of system capabilities and how they react to the prevailing circumstances. The ongoing world economic crises are affecting every country in the world. Although affected by this economic crunch, China sustained its economic growth rate due to its efficient work system capabilities.

China and India accept the challenges of globalization vis a vis outsourcing, environment, poverty, and increased interconnectedness and adapt themselves accordingly. Both are two significant players in the region. They know their responsibilities and obligations to adjust themselves in the community of nations. They are competing in economic, political, and social domains. In the twenty-first century, they are trying to increase their resources for future generations. Good governance and sustainable human development demand such socio-political and economic development by the countries of the modern world. It has been learned during the research that China and India have different forms of government and ideologies.

Their economic and political developments are creeping up regardless of any form of government and ideology. It shows that forms of government and any specific ideology do not hamper development. Although there have been some shocks and setbacks in the form of the Mumbai attacks in 2008 and ethnic riots in Xinjiang, Urumqi, the Muslim majority province in 2009, it slowed down the pace of economic development but did not halt the same owing to the prudential decisions of both governments.

The most vital link in the socio-political and economic systems of a country has always been the economy of the country that flourishes with the participation of skillful social capital. The political system and its institutions take second place in the development of a country. The third and last place is of a social milieu. In the case of China and India, we saw that the West strongly influences both countries and is imitating the same, condoning their norms, values, and customs. Their social systems are a real threat in this age of globalization as they have a lopsided development in this perspective.

Absolute acculturation (total absorption of values of other cultures) has never been a good thing for any society. It is always good for a society to adopt good norms and values of any system to enrich its culture and develop its social systems. China and India are taking most of the bad things from the Western cultures, like popular music and fast food. Such norms and values have increased dissatisfaction on the part of the young generation, and older people are getting depressed owing to the increase in broken families. That has always been a chief characteristic of Eastern or Asian countries. India is making headway in Bollywood by disseminating its culture worldwide. India and China have to take care while imitating the chic of the West.

The East India Company came to the subcontinent after the War of Plassey in 1757 and occupied East Bengal and the whole of India after the War of Independence in 1857. That was one international company, but now there have been thousands of MNCs ruling over the world since 1757. Suppose we evaluate what this study suggests to the world. It gives the following equation:

$$\text{Globalization} = \text{Equity} = \text{Universalism} = \text{Peace}$$

The West does not have this form of equation. The question arises: Can any system give an accurate picture of the said equation? The answer is simple: Islam does. In the operational domain, there seems to be no operationalization of Islam or democracy in the world. The West lacks objectivity in its attitude, and Muslims with the Islamic system lack Ijtihad, a dynamic force for a universal system. Consequently, the following equation is pervasive in the modern world:

$$\text{Globalization} = \text{Inequality} = \text{terrorism} = \text{Disintegration}$$

Naturally, inequality and imbalance in the industrial West and populous South do not have equal distribution of sources and resources between urban and rural peoples and keep them vertically divided. India seems successful, but it has to beware of the people in the deprived territories, which can counterattack at any time.

Relative deprivation and migration of dreams can wake deprived people against the haves. If India intends to make permanent progress, she has to redress the problems of the people living in Kashmir, Punjab, Khalistan, Bengal, and other parts of India where ethnic groups are not satisfied. Internal satisfaction of people with low incomes or have-nots is sine qua non for perennial development in all sectors that may give internal harmony to the system.

Economic fruits should be delivered pragmatically to the grassroots level. As far as political globalization is concerned, India is very vulnerable under the present government. Recent American-Indian defense pact and civil nuclear deal have restricted India from going into an energy deal with Iran's gas pipeline through Pakistan. It shows the Indian government is still under a neocolonial impression even in the twenty-first century. India must be bold in policymaking and recall the immense power of her independent status.

'Horizontal' and 'vertical cleavages'[1] in both societies (China and India) are increasing daily as ethnic, religious, and parochial differences increase, and the everlasting lacuna between the rich and the poor rises at an alarming ratio. The incidents of the Babri Mosque, the Hyderabad mass killing, the Gujarat massacre, and the Mumbai attacks are pertinent examples of increasing ethnic differences in India. In Urumqi (Xinjiang), which is a Muslim-majority province, ethnic riots caused mass killings in China that certainly slowed down economic growth.

It is indispensable for both countries to improve their productivity and efficiency. This should be in all their domain: economic, political, social, environmental, military, and foreign offices. India comprises 16.7 percent of the world's population. Its natural sources are depleting daily and increasing pressure upon the country's political and economic elite to make wise policies. With a land area of 2.0 percent of the world, it has to work hard to sustain an excellent economic growth rate, which is the most important thing for developing a political system.

China has a 30 percent higher population and a three times greater volume in land area than India. Therefore, the day's call for both societies is to be conscientious about sustaining their natural resources. "The need for greater efficiency in managing natural resources like land, water, and minerals has become urgent. In a capital-scarce economy like ours, efficient utilization of our capacity becomes even more critical. We need well-trained and highly skilled people for these things to happen. In today's world, competition in any field is competition in knowledge. That is why we need to build institutions of excellence."[2]

The poverty rate in China is less than in India. The Millennium Development Goals (MDGs) of the United Nations, regarding eradicating poverty and hunger, universal education, gender equality, child health, paternal health, combating HIV/AIDS, sustainable environment, and global partnership, call for eliminating poverty and hunger by the end of 2015. China is very much promising to meet the challenge along with all MDGs. The international poverty line says living on less than 1.25 U.S. dollars means touching the extreme poverty line. The WB believes that in 1990, China had a poverty percentage above 60 percent of its population.

In the same year, the Indian poverty percentage was above 51 percent. By 2005, China, in pursuing the MDGs, reduced the poverty percentage to less than 16 percent compared to India, which reduced it to 40 percent. It is said that this poverty will be reduced in India to 25.4 percent by 2015.[3]

In the case of China, it seems that poverty will be nowhere by 2015. India has to be very vigilant regarding uncertain political and economic development. From 1990 to 2005, in 15 years, India reduces poverty by up to 11 percent only because of lopsided political and economic developments in the 1990s. On the other hand, China made a considerable landmark by reducing poverty to 44 percent in the same period.

This poverty may increase in 2015 if India keeps escalating boundary conflicts with its neighbors. The arms race in the region can cut development projects in India and deprive it of the MDG 2015 targets. India has to make independent decisions by keeping itself separate from joining the American bloc. It is in the national interest of the U.S., not of India.

There are many sources about the reduction of poverty in China and India. From 1981 to 2001, the poverty rate in rural areas where people used to live on less than $1 a day declined from 79 to 27 percent in China and 63 to 42 percent in India.[4] Therefore, it gives the impression that India and China are taking advantage of globalization.

The economic growth rate is significant for measuring the development of any country. According to Baldev Raj Nayyer,[5] India's economy has improved due to globalization. In the pragmatic sense, India was far behind in economic growth before liberalization. For example, from 1956 to 1975, its economic growth rate was only 3.4 percent and went down from 1965 to 1975 by 2.6 percent while liberalization started taking place in India. After liberalizing its economy, India entered the age of globalization successfully and made an economic growth rate of more than 5.5 percent. From 1995 to 2007, economic growth surpassed 6.5 percent, and amazingly, in 2007 to date, India achieved a respectable figure of 8 percent.[6]

In China, the situation is more optimistic; in the literature on political economy, only environmental concerns are considered at stake, while other aspects always look prosperous in the age of globalization. One aspect is that the social system of China is declining very rapidly, as Mr. General Luo Peisen conceded during his interview with the researcher.

Pranab Bardhan[7] thinks, "Issues like globalization, inequality, poverty, and social discontent are thus much more complicated than are allowed in the standard accounts about China and India."[8] The facts discussed in this research illustrate that globalization does not enhance inequality worldwide. Still, it is leadership and government that employ the system's capabilities according to their peculiarities and make a difference in the socio-political and economic development of the country. Second, inequality again occurs when few people in the developed world can go anywhere, and most people are deprived of the same. This inequality is against the MDGs of the U.N.

Therefore, it is not the form of government that makes a difference in a country's socio-political and economic systems. Still, these are individuals of the country who contribute to the progress and prosperity of the state by making the system's capabilities move with their skills and hard work instead of keeping them stagnant. In India, people think it is at a loss in the age of globalization, while in China, most people believe that it does not need to think even about the consequences of globalization; it has accumulated the fruits so far without looking back.

India has an edge over China regarding democracy.

Although democracy still exists in its nascent form in China, it has to adopt it. India should materialize a big difference as early as possible. India can't reduce poverty and attain the MDGs by 2015 without resolving its conflicts with its neighbors. It has to be practical and realistic in its policy-making rather than adopting obstinacy and stubbornness. Obduracy, stubbornness, and blame games for point scoring are unsuitable for democratic values.

India is a regional power; it has to behave accordingly to lead from the front in the region. Information technology is another domain in which India is far ahead of China. It has the most significant software market in the world in Bangalore. Information technology is a source of sustained effectiveness in the globalized world. It all works when there is peace and tranquility at home. It only comes through integrating the deprived communities at the domestic level and enjoying good relations with neighbors.

Chinese labor is more disciplined and cheaper than Indian labor; therefore, there is more investment in China. The Chinese are responding to globalization more effectively than the Indians. Foreign investors always prefer to go to a peaceful country. China has been more peaceful than India.

Testing the Hypotheses

Testing the very first hypothesis of the thesis is related to the status of "system capabilities," considering it more important in the socio-political and economic growth of a country rather than the forms of government. Most independent and dependent factors in social sciences overlap according to the circumstances. An interdisciplinary approach also plays a vital role in determining the success rate of the political system.

Forms of government and system capabilities coordinate to develop a stable political system. Natural calamities perform their role and affect every aspect of human life, even in the presence of efficient system capabilities and democratic norms and values. Thus, it all depends on the individuals of society and how much they participate and are interested in developing their country after any unfortunate event. The people's leadership and behavior construct system capabilities on efficient lines and create a form of government to harmonize their lives.

The second hypothesis is related to the fact that India is a democratic country, and China is a communist one, but globalization is more favorable to China than India. It is deduced that the Indian system's capabilities remain absent owing to its so-called democratic system, and it cannot attain the fruits of globalization as properly as China did. Interestingly, it is observed in China that it has to open up its economy and political system to adjust itself to the phenomenon of increased interconnectedness. This openness is a democratic value. Therefore, democratic norms and values are essential for sustainable development to achieve the end product.

The third hypothesis tells us that the MNCs are consciously giving way to Chinese consumer goods in world trade so that they may become more open and start pragmatically following the rules and regulations of the market economy. China's membership in the WTO covertly adopted the principles of a mixed economy to sustain its economic growth rate to double digits. Hence, it is proved that interdependence is indispensable for any form of government.

The fourth hypothesis regarding the decline in Chinese and Indian cultures while imitating the West and losing their traditional and cultural values is correct, as Chinese social scientists accepted it during their interviews. In the case of India, TV channels support the hypothesis convincingly. After testing the hypotheses, here are the lessons that can be learned from China and India.

Battling with the COVID-19 pandemic testifies to the first hypothesis. We observed that Chinese system capabilities efficiently wrestle with the coronavirus compared to India.

Lessons for Pakistan and other Developing Countries

Pakistan is located in South Asia and has a very significant geographical location. China in the North and India in the East are located. Pakistan can learn a lot of lessons from both of its neighbors. China's hard work and participation of the people in the country's economic development guides Pakistan for future progress. India's leadership made prudent decisions by liberalizing its economy.

China started joint ventures with the MNCs and grew its economy with the outside world's help. It also enjoys a favorable balance of trade and balance of payment by reducing its imports and increasing its exports. Pakistan has to learn that it should develop rules and regulations for the MNCs to sustain local businesses. The MNCs should not be given a free hand for their activities, causing a threat to our environment. Joint ventures where sustain the local economy but also eliminate the chances of monopoly of the MNCs in the country.

China has successfully bridged the gap between the rural and urban elite; therefore, Pakistan should learn how to follow suit through the political elite. India can also learn the same thing from China as it could not achieve that goal yet. Ethnic movements in India may cause secession. The incident of Urumqi, Xinjiang, shows that ethnic riots only cause the killing of innocent and breed hatred against the country, slowing down economic growth. Pakistan should purge all ethnic differences to save its existence. India has learned the Machiavellian strategy how not to be good? Pakistan has to learn to be good but utilize the same according to prevailing circumstances. So-called secularism in India has made it unpopular in world politics and slows down its economic development. Pakistan has to avoid such a situation and give way to tolerance and respect for other communities to promote integration.

Pakistan's military also needs to learn from India how to work within its limits by separating itself from politics. It has to use its strategies and power to defend the country's borders against any impending danger rather than taking military actions against fellow citizens. Pakistan has to preserve its values and social system. It only has to take good things from neighbors, avoiding the otherwise.

The developing world can also learn from China and India that without undermining the social system, they can develop their economy through hard work, democracy, human rights, religious tolerance, and prudent leadership that lead any country to sustainable economic development. Both China and India are found guilty of observing human rights, democracy, and religious tolerance. Lessons can be learned by either adopting good ways or evading evil ways.

Endnotes

1 Rupert Emerson uses terms in his *From Empire to Nations* and Talukder Maniruzzaman in *his National Integration and Political Development in Pakistan*, published in 1967 by the University of California Press.

2 Dr. C. Rangarajan, Responding to Globalization: India's Answer, 4th Ramanbhai Patel Memorial Lecture on Excellence of Education, New Delhi, February 26, 2006.

3 http://timesofindia.indiatimes.com/NEWS/India/World-Bank-paints-a-bleak-picture-of-India-on-poverty/articleshow/4521286.cms. Website accessed on 13-09-09.

4 Pranab Bardhan, Does Globalization Help or Hurt the World's Poor? http://www.sciam.com/article.cfm?chanID=sa006&articleID=0004B7FD-C4E6-1421-84E683414B7F0101. Website visited on 01-01-2008.

5 He is an Emeritus Professor of political science at McGill University, Montreal, writes in his article titled India: Poverty Retreats with Globalization's Advance

6 Baldev Raj Nayyer, India: Poverty Retreats with Globalization's Advance http://yaleglobal.yale.edu/display.article?id=9819. Website visited on 01-01-2008.

7 Pranab Bardhan is a professor of economics at the University of California, Berkeley.

8 Pranab Bardhan, *Inequality in India and China: Is Globalization to Blame?* YaleGlobal, October 15, 2007. http://yaleglobal.yale.edu/display.article?id=9819. Website visited on 01-01-2008.

Index

Acknowledgments

I want to express my sincere appreciation to all those who have helped me to finish this book on *Globalization and System Capabilities: China and India in the Twenty-First Century*. The journey of researching and writing this work has been challenging and rewarding, and I am indebted to the individuals and institutions that have supported me.

First and foremost, I sincerely appreciate my advisor, Dr. Rukhsana A. Siddique, professor at the School of Politics and International Relations, and mentor, Professor Dr. Hamid Hassan Kizzilbash, Professor of Political science, University of the Punjab Lahore. whose guidance and expertise have been invaluable.

I am thankful to two of my students, Dr. Usman Askari, associate professor at the University of Central Punjab, and Dr. Bushra Fatima, assistant professor adjunct in the Bahauddin Zakariya University Multan, who not only incorporated the amendments that came from peer-reviewed sessions but also included the material and literature we provided them to update this book to the contemporary environment. This herculean task was unimaginable without their proactive cooperation.

I want to recognize the scholars, experts, and academics who shared their knowledge and perceptions during interviews, discussions, and collaborative efforts. Their contributions have enriched the depth and breadth of the analysis presented in this book.

I am grateful to the libraries, archives, and research institutions that provided access to essential resources and materials, enabling me to delve into the intricacies of globalization and system capabilities in China and India. I am also thankful to Mr. Shamshad Ahmad Khan, former foreign secretary of Pakistan, who arranged a Chinese visa and scheduled interviews with different sociopolitical and economic think tanks in China. It would have been impossible without help and coordination. I am also indebted to China's Pakistan embassy staff, who graciously welcomed me.

Special thanks go to my kin for their untiring sustenance and considerate patience during the demanding phases of writing. Their reassurance and patience have been a constant source of inspiration.

I thank the publishing team for their dedication and professionalism in bringing this work to fruition. Their commitment to excellence has been instrumental in transforming the manuscript into a comprehensive and coherent publication.

Thank you to everyone who played a part in making this book a reality.

Rana Eijaz Ahmad
Mahnoor Mansoor

About the Authors

Rana Eijaz Ahmad has a Ph.D. in international relations specializing in international political economy. He is one of the senior professors in the Department of Political Science and was a Host Director at the Confucius Institute Punjab University Lahore from 2017 to 2023. Professor Ahmad wrote a book, *Globalization and its Impact on Pakistan*, in 2004. The Oslo University College, Norway, borrowed two chapters 1 and 3 (60 pages) of Professor Ahmad's book *Globalization and its Impact on Pakistan* for the syllabus of Journalism and Communication in the Era of Globalization and Transformation. Professor Ahmad also delivered lectures at the State University of New York campuses. One is at the University at Buffalo, Cora P. Maloney College. The Second lecture was at Buffalo State College, U.S.A. The third lecture was at the West Virginia University Morgan Town, USA. He also translated a novel, *Samarkand*, from English to Urdu. He supervised many theses at the M.A., MPhil, and PhD levels. Professor Ahmad has represented Pakistan on more than 20 occasions in different parts of the world. He edits a Politics and International Studies journal published at the University of Punjab Lahore.
ranaeijaz@gmail.com

Mahnoor Mansoor is a PhD scholar at the Department of Political Science, University of the Punjab Lahore, Pakistan. She is the Chief Executive Officer of a Pakistani-based think tank on Public Policy and Sustainable Governance. She has written four research papers; the other four are being published. She is an adjunct faculty member in public and private sector Pakistani universities. She is also editing a research journal named *Pakistan Political Science Review*.
mahnooreijaz11@gmail.com